Microsoft® Windows Me

Millennium Edition

Copyright - Editions ENI - December 2000
ISBN: 2-7460-1090-9
Original edition: ISBN: 2-7460-1120-4

ENI Publishing LTD

500 Chiswick High Road
London W4 5RG

Tel: 020 8956 2320
Fax: 020 8956 2321

e-mail: publishing@ediENI.com
http://www.eni-publishing.com

Editions ENI

BP 32125
44021 NANTES Cedex 1

Tel: 33.2.51.80.15.15
Fax: 33.2.51.80.15.16

e-mail: editions@ediENI.com
http://www.editions-eni.com

Straight to the Point collection directed by Corinne HERVO

Foreword

The aim of this book is to let you find rapidly how to perform any task in **Windows Millennium Edition** (Windows ME).

Each procedure is described in detail and illustrated so that you can put it into action easily.

The final pages are given over to an **index** of the topics covered and an **appendix**, which give details of shortcut keys.

The typographic conventions used in this book are as follows:

Type faces used for specific purposes:	
bold	indicates the option to take in a menu or dialog box.
italic	is used for notes and comments.
[Ctrl]	represents a key from the keyboard; when two keys appear side by side, they should be pressed simultaneously.

Symbols indicating the content of a paragraph:	
▓	an action to carry out (activating an option, clicking with the mouse...).
⇨	a general comment on the command in question.
🖱	a technique which involves the mouse.
⌨	a keyboard technique.
📃	a technique which uses options from the menus.

🔖 OVERVIEW

🔖 EXPLORER

🔖 APPLICATIONS

⊞ *Windows Millennium Edition*

🔲 CONFIGURATION

APPENDIX

INDEX

Windows Millennium Edition

Windows Millennium Edition

1.1 The working environment

A-Windows Me

When you start your PC, the **Enter Network Password** dialog box may appear. If this is the case, enter your user name and your password (if you have one). The **User name** identifies you within the network. It should be unique within the group of computers (or domain) to which you belong. The **Password** identifies you as that user.

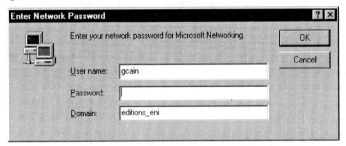

Click **OK**.

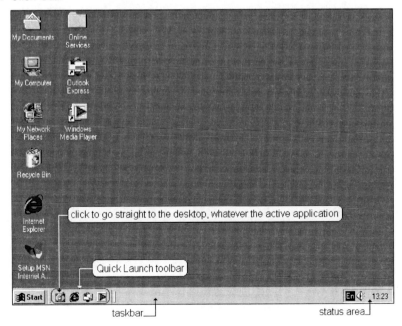

The workspace that appears on the screen is known as the desktop.

It should contain the following:

- the **taskbar**: this is an easy way into the tasks (or active applications). When your computer is first switched on, this bar shows the time and contains the **Start** button which allows you to display the main Windows menu. On the left you can also see the **Quick Launch** toolbar and on the right the **status area**, which usually contains the regional settings indicator, the volume control and the clock.
- the desktop also contains various objects symbolised by icons: the **My Documents** folder is a shortcut to the folder called **My Documents** generally located in C: drive; **My Computer** gives you quick access to the various drives on your computer as well as the **Control Panel**; **My Network Places** shows all the computers, printers and shared resources on the network where you are connected; the **Recycle Bin** is a storage space for deleted files, which allows you to retrieve documents that you may have deleted by mistake; the **Internet Explorer** icon starts the Internet Explorer 5.0 Web browser so you can navigate on the Internet; **My Briefcase** may appear, to allow you to work on files from home or outside your network; the **Online Services** folder, if it appears, provides links to Internet service providers; other objects such as shortcuts to other applications or files may also appear on the desktop.

➪ *If you point to the time on the taskbar, your computer's control date appears.*

The Start menu

Click the **Start** button or press ⌈Ctrl⌋⌈Esc⌋ to show the main menu.

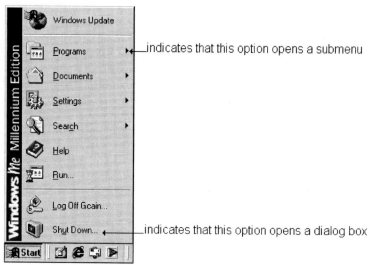

indicates that this option opens a submenu

indicates that this option opens a dialog box

■ To open a submenu, point to the corresponding menu option.

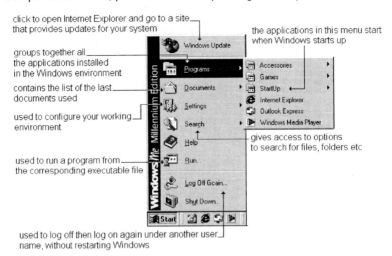

click to open Internet Explorer and go to a site
that provides updates for your system

the applications in this menu start
when Windows starts up

groups together all
the applications installed
in the Windows environment

contains the list of the last
documents used

used to configure your working
environment

gives access to options
to search for files, folders etc

used to run a program from
the corresponding executable file

used to log off then log on again under another user
name, without restarting Windows

■ To close the **Start** menu, click anywhere on the desktop or press ⌨Esc as
many times as necessary.

⇨ *If the **Use Personalized Menus** option is active, infrequently-used applications in the **Programs** menu are hidden: to go to these programs, click
the black arrow that appears at the bottom of this menu.*

B-Starting an application

■ Open the **Start** menu then the menu or submenu containing the application.

■ Click (once) the name of the application.

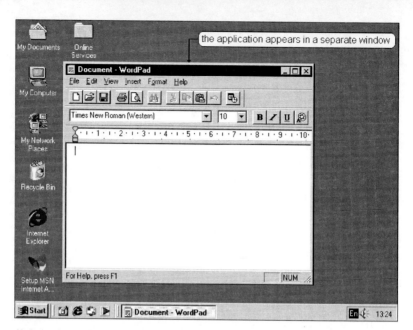

the application appears in a separate window

⇨ *If there is a shortcut on the Quick Launch bar, click the shortcut once to start the application. A shortcut may exist on the desktop: in this case, double-click the shortcut to start the application.*

C-Leaving an application

▨ To leave an application, shut its window:

| File | ⊠ | Alt F4 |
| Exit |

▨ If you need to, save the last changes in the active document.

⇨ *If the application window is minimised, right-click the corresponding button then choose* **Close**.

D-Using Windows help

▨ Open the **Start** menu and activate the **Help** option.

▨ On the **Home** page, click one of the links in the left side of the window then click the link for the subject that interests you. Next, click the help topic you wish to consult (this has a question mark in front of it) or click a link that will take you to a Web page on the Microsoft site (these links have an Internet Explorer 5.5 icon in front of them) and read the help text offered.

enter keywords to search the help pages

use to scroll through the help pages

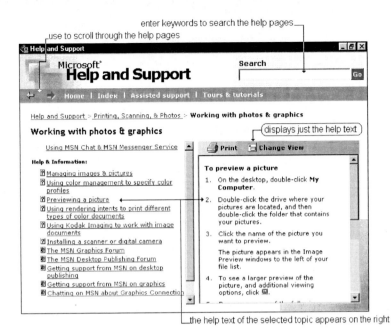

the help text of the selected topic appears on the right

▨ On the **Index** page, enter the start of the keyword by which you want to search then double-click the topic that interests you to see the corresponding help text.

▨ The **Assisted support** page can be used to consult the Microsoft online help, to submit problems or to exchange information via forums and e-mail.

▨ The **Tours & tutorials** page gives you access to presentations of various Windows Me features.

▨ To print a help text, make your search then click [🖨 **Print**] and click **OK**.

E-Turning off the computer

▨ Click the **Start** button then click **Shut Down**.

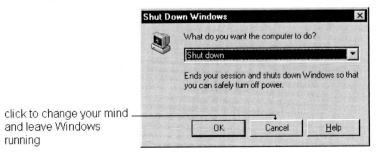

click to change your mind and leave Windows running

- Check that the **Shut down** option appears in the **What do you want the computer to do?** list box then click **OK**.
- If necessary, save changes made to any open files.

1.2 Managing windows

A-Description of the various windows

- There are two types of window: **application windows**, which contain an application's menu bar and toolbars. Some applications, such as Word or Excel, allow you to open several documents simultaneously; in this case, each document appears in its own **document window**. Each window contains the following elements:

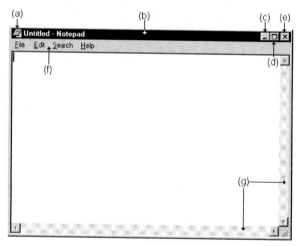

(a)	the **Control Menu** button used to manage the size and position of the window, or to close it.
(b)	a **title bar** displaying the name of the active document (here it says **Untitled**, because the open document has never been saved) followed by the name of the application.
(c)/(d)	The **Minimize** and **Maximize** buttons: the first reduces the window to an icon on the taskbar, and the second allows it to fill the whole screen.
(e)	the **Close** button which you use to close the window and leave the application.
(f)	the **menu bar** contains the application's various menus (these are closed in the illustration).

(g) the **scroll bars and arrows** are used to scroll the contents of the window (here they appear dim, because the window is empty).

B-Moving a window

▨ Point to the window's title bar.

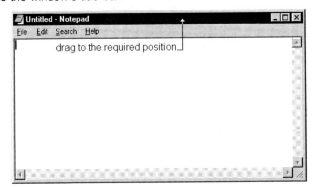

C-Resizing a window

▨ To enlarge a window so that it takes up the whole screen, click the button on the window's title bar.

If it is an application window, it takes up the whole screen: only the taskbar remains (although that too can be hidden). If it is a document window, it takes up all the available space within the corresponding application window.

▨ To bring the window back to its original size, click the button.

▨ To change the width <u>or</u> the height of a window, point to the corresponding edge. To modify both the height <u>and</u> the width, point to one of the corners of the window and drag.

▨ To make the window as small as possible while still keeping the application active, click the button or click the corresponding button on the taskbar:

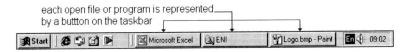

▨ To open one of the windows minimised on the taskbar, simply click its name.

D-Managing more than one window

▓ When you have two overlapping windows on your screen, you can tell the one which is active by its coloured title bar; the corresponding button on the taskbar appears pressed in.

▓ To go into a window (and activate the application), click the window. If it is not visible, click the application's button on the taskbar.

You can also press Alt *and* ⇄ *together as many times as it takes to activate the window you want.*

▓ To change the arrangement of the windows, right-click an empty space in the taskbar to display the bar's menu. Choose one of these three options:

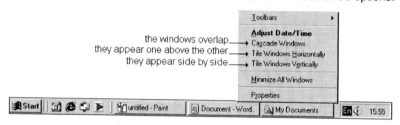

▓ To minimise all the windows, show the taskbar menu and activate the **Minimize All Windows** option.

▓ It is possible to cancel this action by activating the **Undo Minimize All Windows** option in the taskbar menu.

E-Closing a window

▓ Click the ☒ button, or press Alt F4 for an application window, Ctrl F4 for a document windows.

➪ *To close the window is to leave the application: if one of the documents has not been saved, Windows prompts you to save it before closing the window.*

➪ *In an application window, you can use the File - Exit command to leave the application.*

F-Managing menus and options

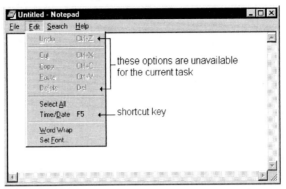 ▦ Click the name of the menu you want to open.

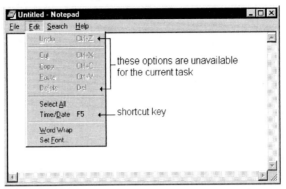

- these options are unavailable for the current task
- shortcut key

▦ To open a menu to the left or right of the open menu, simply point to that menu's name.

▦ To activate an option in the menu, point to the option (do not click until the pointer is on the option) then click.

▦ To close a menu without taking one of the options, click anywhere in the window outside the menu.

▦ To access the menu bar, type Alt or F10.

The first menu is selected, but not open.

▦ To select the menu to the left or the right of the current selection, press → or ←.

▦ To open a selected menu, press Enter or ↓.

▦ To open a menu directly, hold down the Alt key as you press the shortcut letter underlined in the menu's name.

▦ To activate an option, type the shortcut letter (do not press Enter).

▦ To close a menu, without taking an option, press Esc or Alt or F10.

⇨ *To open a shortcut menu (a condensed menu with options pertaining to the selected item), right-click the item concerned.*

G-Using dialog boxes

▓ Dialog boxes contain some or all of the following items:

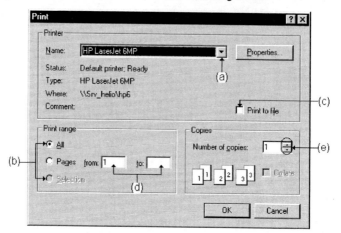

(a)   this is known as a **drop-down list**: to open the list and select an option (or alternatively to close the list), click the ▼ button (on the keyboard, you need to access the list then press Alt ↓).

(b)   the active option is the one whose **option button** appears filled in. In a single options group (as seen here in the Print range frame), only one option can be active.

(c)   the option is active if the **check box** is ticked.

(d)   you use a **text box** to enter data; when the data required is numerical, the text box may contain **increment buttons** (e) which you can click to increase or decrease the value displayed.

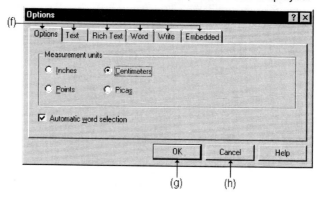

(f)   **tabs** are used to move between different pages in a dialog box.

(g)   the **OK** button closes the dialog box and confirms any changes you may have made to options.

(h)   the **Cancel** button closes the dialog box, cancelling any changes you may have made (clicking the ☒ button has a similar effect).

▨ To activate another page in the dialog box, click the tab concerned.

▨ On the keyboard, use ⇄ or ⇧ Shift ⇄ to move between options. To go directly to a specific option or group of options, press Alt and the shortcut letter. Within a group of options or a list use the arrow keys to move around. A check box is activated and deactivated by the space bar. To cancel your latest modifications to the options and leave the dialog box, press Esc.

⇨ *The* ? *button activates on-line help so that you can obtain explanations of the various options (you can also display help texts by right-clicking an option, and selecting **What's this?**).*

2.1 The Explorer window

A-Starting the Windows Explorer

▦ **Start - Programs - Accessories - Windows Explorer**

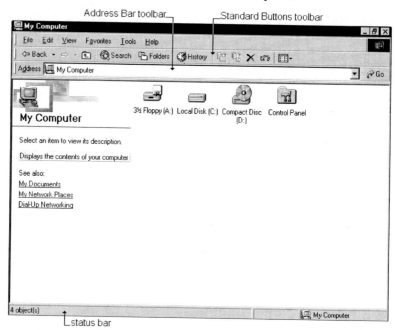

▦ To show (or hide) the status bar, activate (or deactivate) the corresponding option in the **View** menu. To show (or hide) a toolbar, activate (or deactivate) the corresponding option in **View - Toolbars**.

⇨ *When you double-click the **My Documents**, **My Computer**, **My Network Places** or **Recycle Bin** shortcuts or if you activate for example the command **Start - Settings - Control Panel**, you open windows similar to the Windows Explorer that directly show details of the file or item concerned.*

⇨ *You can also start the Windows Explorer by right-clicking the **Start** button and activating the **Explore** option.*

B-Going into a drive/folder

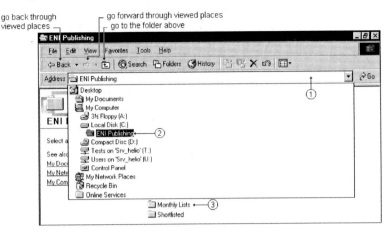

go back through viewed places

go forward through viewed places

go to the folder above

① Open this drop-down list to see all the elements from the desktop.

② Click the item you wish to explore.

③ To go to a folder, double-click its icon.

⇨ *All of these options can also be found in the* **View** *-* **Go To** *menu.*

⇨ *To update the contents of a window (if changes have occurred since it has been on the screen), use* **View** *-* **Refresh** *or* F5 .

⇨ *To go to a Web page while in the Explorer, enter its address in the* **Address Bar** *and press* Enter *to confirm.*

C-Presenting the list of folders/files

To define the list's presentation, choose one of these five options from the **View** menu or use the ⊞▾ button:

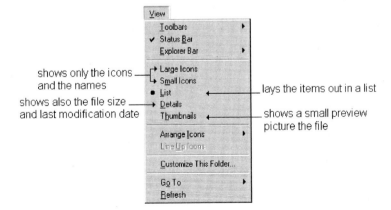

shows only the icons and the names

shows also the file size and last modification date

lays the items out in a list

shows a small preview picture the file

*When you choose **Details** layout, the following elements appear:*

drag to adjust ⎯⎯⎯⎯⎯ the column width

click once or twice to sort the column contents in ascending or descending order

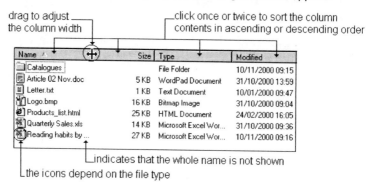

└ indicates that the whole name is not shown

└ the icons depend on the file type

▓ To sort the list of files and folders, use **View - Arrange Icons**.

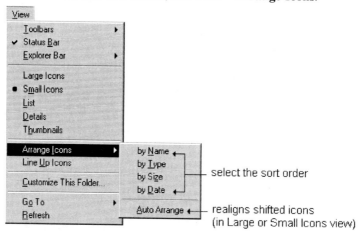

select the sort order

realigns shifted icons
(in Large or Small Icons view)

⇨ *In **Details** layout, you can choose columns to show particular types of information with the **View - Choose Columns** command.*

D-Showing the image preview

▨ Go to the **My Pictures** folder which is stored in the **My Documents** folder.

① Click the picture in question.

② Use the following buttons:

(a)　　to zoom in on the picture.

(b)　　to zoom out.

(c)　　to show a larger preview of the image; click ☒ to close the window.

(d)　　to show the picture at its actual size.

(e)　　to show the picture at its best possible size.

(f)　　to print the picture.

(g)　　to rotate the picture.

⇨ *If you wish to use the image preview in a folder other than the **My Pictures** folder, activate the folder and use **View - Customize This Folder**. Click the **Next** button then activate the **Choose or edit an HTML template for this folder** option and click **Next**. In the **Choose a template** list, activate the **Image Preview** option then click **Next** and finally **Finish**.*

E-Using the Folders explorer bar

▨ If necessary, display the **Folders** explorer bar with **View - Explorer Bar - Folders** or click the [⌐Folders] button.

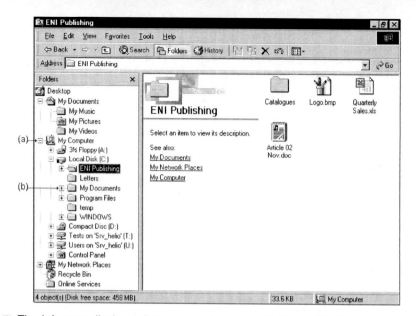

- The left pane displays all the elements on the **Desktop**: **My Documents**, **My Computer**, **My Network Places**, **Recycle Bin** and possibly **Online Services** and **My Briefcase**. The right pane displays the list of items (files or folders) contained in the element selected on the left.

- The different desktop elements are presented in a hierarchical form. Some branches of the hierarchy are expanded (a) showing the folders and files they contain while others (b) are collapsed.

  An expanded branch is symbolised by a - sign; a collapsed branch displays a + sign. To collapse or expand a branch, simply click the - or + sign.

- To see the contents of an element or folder, click it in the left pane.

- To expand a branch completely, click that branch then type *.

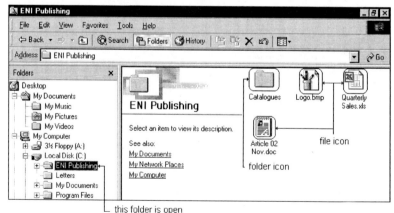

⇨ *When a folder appears in the right pane, double-click the folder icon (and not its name) to see its contents.*

F- Using the History explorer bar

▒ If necessary, show the **History** bar with one of these commands:

View Ctrl **H**
Explorer Bar
History
By default, the left pane shows a list of the HTML pages or files sorted by the date visited.

▒ To see the files opened on a specific day or week, click that day or week.

▒ Click the site containing the pages that you want to see.

▒ To see an html page in the right side of the screen, click its name.

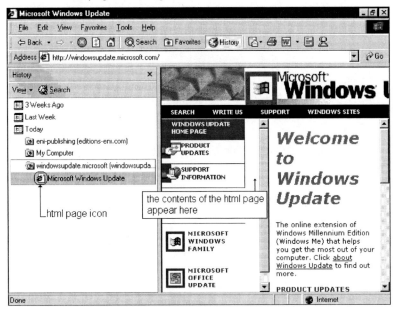

▒ If you click a page associated with another icon, the application where the file was created starts and displays the chosen file.

▒ To modify how history items are listed, click the **View** button on the **History** bar.

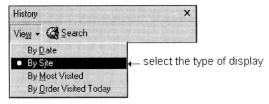

← select the type of display

To search in the **History** bar:

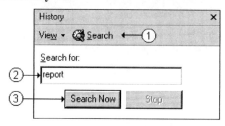

① Click this button.

② Enter the start of the name, or the whole name of the page you wish to find.

③ Click to start the search.

To close the **Search** pane of the **History** bar, click the **View** button and choose a view type for the **History** bar.

G-Using the Favorites explorer bar

You use Favorites mainly to access frequently visited Web pages more rapidly.

If necessary, display the **Favorites** bar with one of the following:
View - Explorer Bar - Favorites or Ctrl I

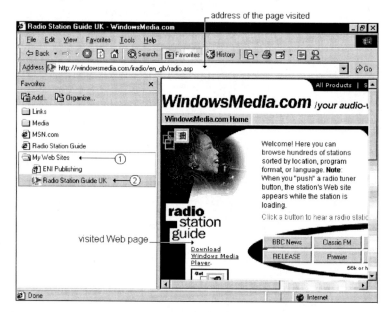

① Click the name of the folder (and subfolder if appropriate) containing the Web page you wish to see.

② Click the page name.

Adding a Web page to the Favorites

▓ In the **Address Bar**, enter the Web page address then press Enter : the page contents appear on the right side of the screen.

▓ **Favorites - Add to Favorites** or Add...

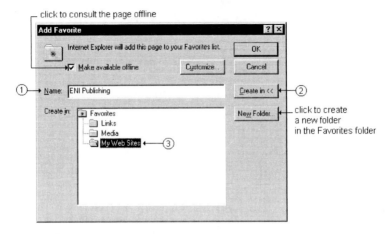

① Enter the name of the page.

② If necessary, click this button.

③ Specify where you wish to save the Web page.

Organising the Favorites folder

▓ **Favorites - Organize Favorites** or Organize...

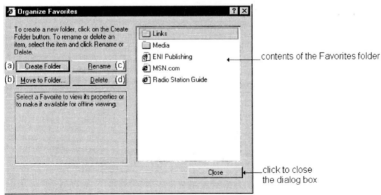

▓ To expand the contents of a subfolder of the **Favorites** folder, click its name in the right side of the dialog box.

- To create a folder, click the name of the folder where the new folder will be stored (if necessary) then click the button (a); enter the name of the new folder and confirm.

- To move a Web page into one of the folders within the **Favorites** folder, click the page name then click the button (b); click the name of the folder where you wish to move the page.

- To rename an item, click its name then click the button (c); enter the new name then press Enter .

- To delete an item from the **Favorites** folder, click its name then click the button (d); confirm sending the item to the **Recycle Bin** by clicking **OK**.

H-Setting the folder view options

- Activate the folder for which you wish to change the view settings.
- **Tools - Folder Options - View** tab

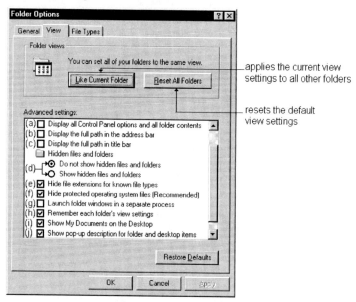

applies the current view settings to all other folders

resets the default view settings

- Activate or deactivate the following options:

(a)   when active, this shows a full list of Control Panel and folder items by default.

(b)   if you deactivate this option, only the name of the item appears in the Address Bar, not its complete file path.

(c)   if you deactivate this option, only the name of the selected item appears in the title bar.

(d)   shows/hides system files and folders in the file list.

(e)   this hides/shows the extensions for each file type.

(f)   hides/shows operating system files.

(g) indicates to Windows that you wish to open each folder in a separate part of the memory.

(h) if this option is active, Windows saves a folder's view options when the folder is closed.

(i) if you deactivate this option, the **My Documents** folder will no longer appear directly on the desktop, whether on the desktop screen or in the file hierarchy.

(j) if this is active, a description of each folder/desktop item to which you point appears in a ScreenTip.

2.2 Managing files and folders

A-Managing file selection

In Double-click mode

The active work mode is Double-click by default, but you can change this if required (cf. Activating Single-click/Double-click mode).

To select several files, point to the empty space just to the right of the first name you wish to select. Drag the mouse until all the required names/icons are enclosed in a dotted rectangle.

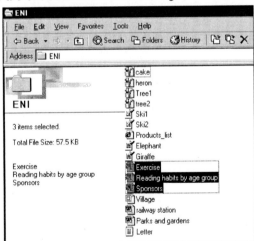

To spread the selection to include adjacent files, hold down `⇧ Shift` and click the last document you wish to include.

To select another group of files, hold down `⇧ Shift` and drag around the new group.

To insert another file in the selection, hold down `Ctrl` and click the file.

To select all the files in the active folder, use **Edit - Select All** or `Ctrl` **A**.

- ▨ To deselect files, hold down ⎡Ctrl⎤ and drag around any files you wish to remove from the selection.
- ▨ To deselect all the files, click anywhere in the window except on a file name.

⇨ *You can also invert the selection using the corresponding option in the* **Edit** *menu.*

⇨ *When a selection has been made, right-click the selection to see a shortcut menu adapted to that selection.*

⇨ *You can also select via the keyboard: go to the first file, hold down* ⎡⇧ Shift⎤ *then use the arrow keys to spread out the selection. To select a non-adjacent file, hold down* ⎡Ctrl⎤ *then use the* ⎡↑⎤ *or* ⎡↓⎤ *keys to reach the file and press* ⎡space⎤ *to select it.*

In Single-click mode

- ▨ To select a file, point to its name or icon.
- ▨ To select several adjacent files, point to the name of the first file (do not click!) hold down ⎡⇧ Shift⎤ then drag the mouse down to the last file you wish to select. Be sure not to move the mouse on to another file or you will deselect your selection! As in double-click mode you can also drag around files to select them.
- ▨ To spread the selection over adjacent files, hold down the ⎡⇧ Shift⎤ key and while holding it point to the last item you wish to add to the selection (take care to point to and not to click the file).
- ▨ To select another group of files without losing the current selection, make sure the mouse is not pointing to another file name, hold down the ⎡Ctrl⎤ key then drag over the files you wish to select; release the ⎡Ctrl⎤ key then the mouse button and move the pointer out of the list.
- ▨ To insert another file into the selection, hold down ⎡Ctrl⎤ and point to the name of the file.
- ▨ To deselect a file, hold down ⎡Ctrl⎤ and point to the name of the file you wish to remove from the selection. Release the ⎡Ctrl⎤ key then make sure you move the pointer out of the list.
- ▨ To deselect a group of adjacent files, hold down ⎡Ctrl⎤ then point to each file you wish to remove from the selection. Release ⎡Ctrl⎤ then move the pointer away from the list of file names.
- ▨ To deselect all the files, click elsewhere in the window apart from the list of files.

⇨ *You can select all the files using the* **Edit - Select All** *command or with* ⎡Ctrl⎤ **A**.

B-Creating a folder

- ▨ Select the folder in which you wish to create a new folder or make sure that this folder's contents are displayed in the Explorer window.
- ▨ **File - New - Folder**

Alternatively, right-click an empty space in the list, and choose the option New then Folder.

▓ Enter the new folder's name: it can be up to 255 characters long, including spaces, and may contain capital letters. It must not contain the characters \ / ? : " < > or |.

▓ Confirm by pressing Enter .

C-Copying folders or files

First method

▓ Select the folders or files you want to copy in the right window pane.

▓ **Edit - Copy to Folder** or [icon]

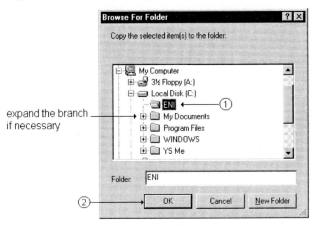

① Click the name of the copy's destination folder. If this is not visible, expand the branch.

② Click to confirm.

Second method

▓ Select the folders or the files concerned.

▓ Copy these files into the clipboard:

Edit - Copy or Ctrl **C**

▓ Select the destination folder.

▓ Paste the clipboard's contents:

Edit - Paste or Ctrl **V**

The files are copied one by one. They are still in the clipboard, so that you can copy them into another folder if you need to.

Third method

▓ Select the folders or files you want to copy.

▓ Make sure that you can see the destination folder in the hierarchy (if it is in another folder, this should be open).

▓ Drag the files or folder to the destination folder; if you are copying onto the same drive, hold down the [Ctrl] key.

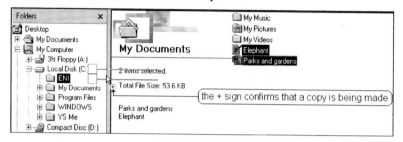

⇨ *You can also drag with the right mouse button then choose* **Copy Here** *in the menu which appears.*

⇨ *To select several folders, you should work in the right pane of the Windows Explorer (and not in the folder hierarchy); when you copy a folder, Windows copies the folder's entire hierarchy including subfolders and the files they contain.*

⇨ *If the destination folder already contains a file of the same name as the one you are copying, Windows will ask if it should overwrite the original file.*

⇨ *If you copy a file into the same folder, Windows creates a duplicate, called* **Copy of** *followed by the file name.*

⇨ *If you copy to a network workstation that does not handle long file names, you must confirm that the first eight characters of the copied file's name can be used for the name of the destination file.*

D-Moving folders or files

First method

▓ Select the files or folders you want to move.

To select several folders, make your selection in the right pane of the Explorer window.

▓ **Edit - Move to Folder** or [icon]

▓ In the **Browse For Folder** dialog box, expand the branch if necessary to click the name of the destination folder then click **OK**.

Second method

▓ Select the files or folders you want to move.

▓ Move the items into the clipboard by using **Edit - Cut** or [Ctrl] **X**.

▓ Select the destination folder.

▓ Use **Edit - Paste** or [Ctrl] **V** to paste the clipboard contents into the folder.

Third method

- Select the files or folders you want to move.
- Drag them to the destination folder: if you are moving them to another drive, hold down [Shift] as you drag.

  When you point to the destination folder, you should not see a + sign next to the pointer.

⇨ *You can also drag the selection with the right mouse button then choose* **Move Here** *in the menu displayed.*

E-Copying folders or files onto a floppy disk

- Check that there is a formatted disk in the drive.
- Select the folders or files concerned.
- Right-click to show the selection's shortcut menu.
- Point to the **Send To** option then click the option corresponding to the floppy disk drive, for example **3 1/2 Floppy (A)**.

⇨ *You can also use one of the methods listed in the "Copying folders or files" section.*

F-Sending files by electronic mail

- Select the file(s) concerned.
- Right-click to show the selection's shortcut menu.
- Point to the **Send To** option and choose **Mail Recipient**.

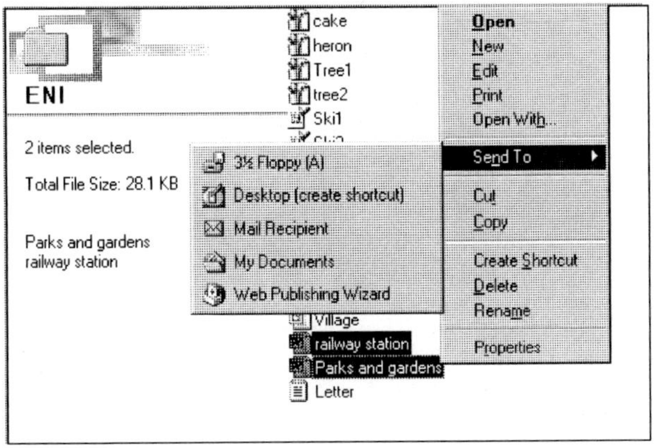

  Windows starts your e-mail application.

- Enter the name(s) of your mail recipient(s) and the subject of your message.
- Send the message.

⇨ *The selected files will be sent as attached files.*

G-Renaming a file or folder

▦ Select the file or folder you want to rename.

▦ Click the name then click the place where you wish to put the insertion point or use the **File - Rename** command.

▦ Use the usual keys for modifying any text then enter.

The name is modified automatically. If the active folder already contains a file of the same name, Windows refuses to rename the file.

⇨ *You can cancel this action with **Edit - Undo Rename** or* Ctrl *Z.*

H-Deleting folders or files

▦ Select the folders or files you wish to delete.

▦ **File**   Del
  Delete

▦ Click **Yes** to confirm sending the items to the Recycle Bin.

⇨ *When you delete a folder, any files or subfolders it contains are also deleted.*

⇨ *The deletion is not final: the files still have a physical existence on the disk but are no longer visible in a folder. To delete the files for good, making space on the disk, remove them from the Recycle Bin, or empty this bin.*

⇨ *You can also delete a file or folder by dragging its icon onto the Recycle Bin icon on the desktop.*

⇨ *Be careful: if you delete from another drive apart from the hard disk (the floppy disk drive or another workstation), the deletion is final and you will not be able to retrieve the items later!*

⇨ *If you would rather not have to confirm each instruction to delete, deactivate the **Display delete confirmation dialog** option in the **Global** tab of the **Recycle Bin Properties** dialog box.*

⇨ *If the files you wish to delete are located in several folders, make a search for them and select them in the **Search** window then delete them.*

⇨ *To delete files from the disk definitively, without sending them to the Recycle Bin first, press* ⇧ Shift Del *instead of just* Del.

I- Managing the files in the Recycle Bin

To view the files, open the **Recycle Bin** by double-clicking its icon on the desktop or open it from the Explorer window.

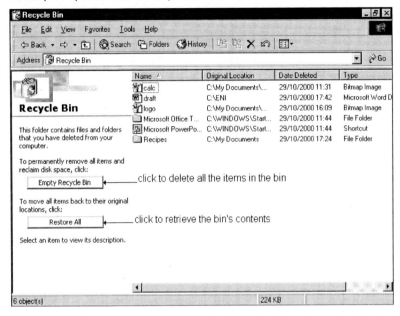

To retrieve one or more files, go to the **Recycle Bin** window and select the file(s) then activate the **File - Restore** command or click the **Restore** button.

*You can also right-click the selection then choose the **Restore** option.*

The file is once again available in the Explorer window. If necessary, Windows recreates the folder which contained the file.

To empty the Recycle Bin, right-click the bin icon then choose **Empty Recycle Bin** or if the corresponding window is open, use the **File - Empty Recycle Bin** command or click the **Empty Recycle Bin** button. Click **Yes** to confirm deleting all the items.

⇨ *The **Recycle Bin** icon on the desktop varies, depending on what it contains: if it is empty, it appears like this:* [image], *otherwise it takes this shape:* [image].

J- Printing files from the Explorer

▓ Select the files concerned.

▓ Right-click the selection and choose the **Print** option.

You can also use the File - Print command.

⇨ *If the printer icon is on the desktop, you can drag the selection onto that icon.*

⇨ *To print the list of files, make a screen capture of the contents of the folder in question then print it from Paint (cf. "Making a screen capture").*

K-Protecting/unprotecting a file

▓ Select the file concerned.

▓ **File - Properties** or Alt Enter

You can also right-click the file and choose Properties.

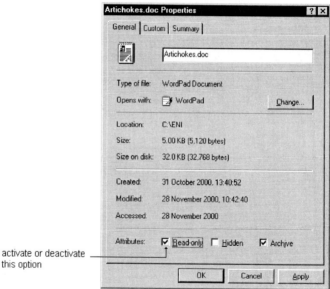

activate or deactivate
this option

⇨ *You will no longer be able to modify the contents of the file. Windows will refuse to save any changes and will automatically request confirmation before deleting a protected document.*

L-Finding files or folders

By name, contents or file location

▧ **Start - Search - For Files or Folders**

You can also access the search window by activating the **Search** *explorer bar in any Explorer window.*

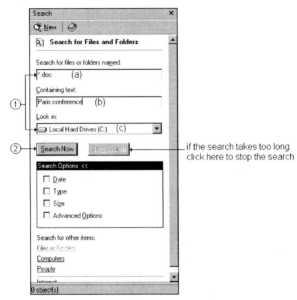

① Set your search criteria in the various boxes given:

(a)   Enter the whole or part of the name you want to find. You can use the wildcard characters * and ?: * represents a string of characters of varying length and ? represents a single character.

(b)   Enter the exact text the files should contain.

(c)   Select the drive or folder where the search should be made or click the **Browse** option to select it.

② Start the search.

The search results (all the files that meet the specified search criteria) appear in the right window pane.

Search Results

File Edit View Favorites Tools Help

⇦ Back ▾ ⇨ ▾ ⬧ | 🔍 Search 📁 Folders 🕒 History | ⬛ ⬛ ✕ ⬦ | ⊞▾

Address 🔍 Search Results ▾ ⬀ Go

Search ✕

🔍 New | ⬧

🔍 **Search for Files and Folders**

Search for files or folders named:
```
*.doc
```

Containing text:
```
Paris conference
```

Look in:
```
💾 Local Hard Drives (C:)  ▾
```

Search Now | Stop Search

Search Options <<

☐ Date
☐ Type
☐ Size
☐ Advanced Options

Search for other items:
Files or Folders
Computers
People
Internet

Search Results

Select an item to view its description.

Report Paris Meeting   European sales   Article 02 Nov

all these files have a .doc extension
and contain the text "Paris conference"

3 object(s) | 334 KB | 💻 My Computer

the number of files found

⇨ *You can select files in the list to copy or move them, etc.*

By date

▦ **Start - Search - For Files or Folders**

▦ If necessary, click **Search Options**.

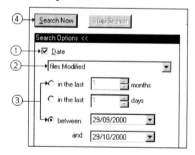

④ → Search Now | Stop Search

Search Options <<

① → ☑ Date
② → files Modified ▾

③ → ◦ in the last [1] months
    ◦ in the last [1] days
    ◉ between [29/09/2000] ▾
    and [29/10/2000] ▾

① Tick this check box.

② Open this drop-down list to determine whether the search should depend on the date the files were last altered (**files Modified**), the date they were created (**files Created**) or the date they were last opened (**files Last Accessed**).

③ Use these option buttons to specify a search over a period of time in months, days or between two dates.

④ Start the search.

By file type or size

▓ **Start - Search - For Files or Folders**

▓ If necessary, click **Search Options**.

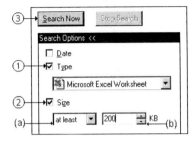

① To search for a particular file type, tick this box then open the drop-down list that appears and make your choice.

② To search according to file size, tick this box. In the drop-down list (a), activate either **at least** or **at most** then give the file size in the text box (b).

③ Start the search.

Setting advanced search criteria

▓ **Start - Search - For Files or Folders**

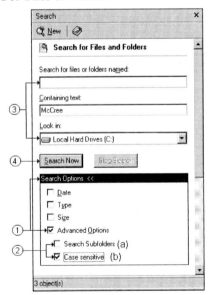

① If necessary, click **Search Options** then tick the **Advanced Options** check box.

② Tick the following options:

(a)   To search the folder indicated in the **Look in** box, including any subfolders it contains.

(b)   To look for the same combination of upper case and lower case letters as entered in the **Containing text** box.

③ Give other search criteria if required.

④ Start the search.

⇨ *If you wish to save search criteria, click in the Search Results pane and use File - Save Search then enter or modify the name for the criteria file (these carry an .fnd extension).*

⇨ *When you wish to use these criteria for a new search, open the corresponding .fnd file with a double-click, modify the criteria if required then start your new search.*

M-Creating a shortcut in the Explorer

▓ Go to the Explorer.

▓ Right-click the file, folder etc to which you wish to create a shortcut (in the right pane of the window if the **Folders** explorer bar is displayed).

▓ Activate the **Create Shortcut** option.

The shortcut is created in the current folder.

▓ Move the shortcut to the required place (another folder or onto the desktop).

⇨ *To delete a shortcut, proceed as for a file. Only the link to the file or folder is deleted, not the item itself.*

N-Opening an application from inside the Explorer

With a program file or a file created with the application

▓ Double-click the icon of the program file or of a document created by the application you wish to open.

⇨ *You can also select the file name and press* Enter *, or activate the Open option in the File menu.*

With any data file

It is possible to start an application with any file created by it, or any file with a format that the application can read.

▓ Double-click the file name, or select it and click with the right mouse button then choose **Open with**.

▓ If Windows suggests the name of the program you wish to use, click it or click the **Choose Program** option.

click to access the disk hierarchy⌐

① Select the program capable of opening the file.

② If you want to establish a permanent association between the document and the program, activate this option.

O-Associating an extension with a program file

Most extension-application associations are predefined in Windows. If your file has an unrecognised extension, you can specify the name of the associated program. To perform this action you need to be the administrator or have administrator permissions.

Creating the association

▓ From the Explorer window, use the **Tools - Folder Options** command.

▓ Click the **File Types** tab.

The list displayed corresponds to the file types visible in the Explorer's detailed lists. Each file type has an extension and is associated with an application.

▓ Click the **New** button.

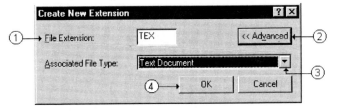

① Enter the extension that you wish to associate with a program.

② Click this button if necessary.

③ Select the associated file type.

④ Click to confirm.

Modifying the association settings

▨ Once the extension has been defined, click the **Advanced** button on the **Folder Options** dialog box to define what action should be carried out when you double-click the icon for a file of this type.

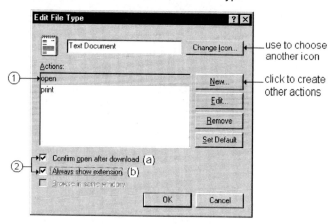

① Select the action that should be carried out when you double-click the file icon in question. If double-clicking should open the application, choose the **open** action.

② Set the following options:

(a) Should Internet Explorer prompt for confirmation before opening this type of file?

(b) If you want this type of file's extension to be displayed, even if the **Hide file extensions for known file types** option in **Tools - Folder Options - View** tab is active.

⇨ *In the Explorer, the File - New command allows you to associate the document you are creating directly with an application by choosing the appropriate option (Microsoft Excel Worksheet, Wave Sound, Bitmap Image etc).*

P-Using a compressed folder

Creating a compressed folder

▨ In the Explorer window, select the drive or folder in which you wish to create your compressed folder.

▨ Use **File - New - Compressed Folder**.

You can also right-click any empty space in the list and choose the New option then Compressed Folder.

▨ Give a name for the compressed folder.

▨ Confirm by pressing ⌨Enter .

Adding files or folders to a compressed folder

▓ Select the files or folders you want to add.

▓ **Edit - Copy** or ⌨Ctrl⌨ **C**

▓ Open the compressed folder in which you wish to add the copied files or folders.

The compressed folder opens in a separate Explorer window.

▓ Paste in the contents of the clipboard with **Edit - Paste** or ⌨Ctrl⌨ **V**.

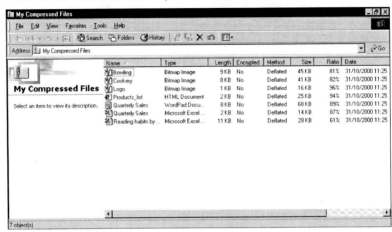

*If you activate the **View - Details** command, you can see the current file size in kilobytes (KB) in the **Length** column, the original file size in the Size column and the file compression percentage in the **Ratio** column.*

⇨ *You can also drag files or folders directly into the compressed folder.*

Extracting one or more files from a compressed folder

When a file is extracted, a decompressed copy is created in another folder or on another drive.

▓ In the compressed folder, select the file(s) concerned.

▓ **Edit - Copy** or ⌨Ctrl⌨ **C**

▓ Select the folder or drive into which the files should be extracted.

▓ **Edit - Paste** or ⌨Ctrl⌨ **V**

⇨ *The files still exist in the compressed folder. You can delete these files by selecting them and pressing* ⌨Del⌨. *You should confirm deletion by clicking* **Yes**.

Extracting all the files or folders from a compressed folder

▓ Select the compressed folder.

▓ **File - Extract All**

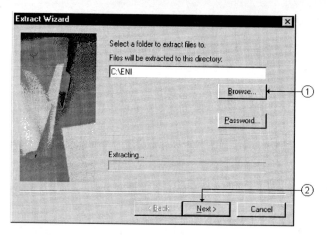

① Choose the folder into which you wish to place the extracted files.

② Click here to go to the next step in the wizard.

▦ Activate the **Show extracted files** option to view the files in the folders into which they have been extracted.

▦ Click the **Finish** button.

⇨ *You can also right-click a compressed folder and choose the* **Extract All** *option.*

⇨ *The extracted files still exist in the compressed folder. You can delete them if you wish.*

Protecting a compressed folder with a password

▦ Open the compressed folder whose contents you wish to protect by means of a password.

▦ **File - Encrypt**

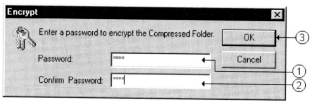

① Enter your password.

② Confirm it by entering it again.

③ Click to confirm.

⇨ *If you activated the* **View - Details** *command, the* **Encrypted** *column contains a* **Yes** *value for all protected files.*

⇨ *If you wish to copy or open an encrypted file, Windows will ask you to enter your* **Password**.

⇨ *To unprotect the folder, open it and choose the **File - Decrypt** command. You will have to supply the **Password** again.*

2.3 Drives

A-Formatting a floppy disk

You cannot use a new disk until you have formatted it. Formatting organises the floppy disk according to the specifications of your computer's drive (in particular, it determines the disk's capacity).

▓ Start from the Explorer, or go into **My Computer** from the desktop. Right-click the icon of the floppy drive.

▓ Click the **Format** option.

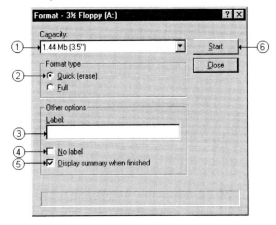

① Define the capacity of the floppy disk: if it is a high density diskette, choose **1.44 Mb**, if it is a low density one, choose **720 Kb**.

② If the disk has been formatted before, you can choose this option: this erases all the files from the disk but does not check the state of the tracks.

③ Give a name for the disk.

④ If you activate this option, the **Label** text box becomes unavailable.

⑤ Leave this option active to obtain a status report for the floppy disk.

⑥ Click to start formatting.

⇨ *Formatting a disk destroys all the files on it.*

B-Changing the label of a drive

▦ Right-click the drive's icon (in the Explorer window, or in My Computer) then click **Properties**.

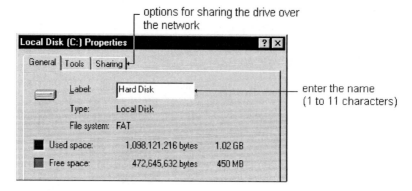

options for sharing the drive over the network

enter the name (1 to 11 characters)

C-Viewing your system's properties

▦ Right-click the **My Computer** icon (on the desktop or in the Explorer window) then click the **Properties** option. You can also go into the **Control Panel** and double-click the **System** icon.

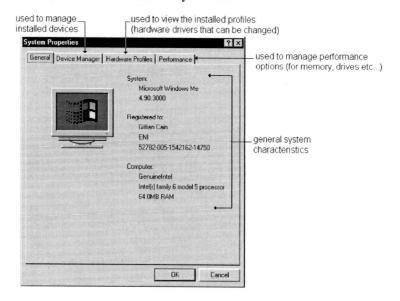

used to manage installed devices

used to view the installed profiles (hardware drivers that can be changed)

used to manage performance options (for memory, drives etc...)

general system characteristics

D-Changing the computer's name

This action is only possible on computers that are part of a network and only if you have network administrator permissions.

▓ Right-click the **My Network Places** icon (on the desktop or in the Explorer window) then choose the **Properties** option. You can also go into the **Control Panel** and double-click the **Network** icon.

▓ Click the **Identification** tab.

▓ Enter the new **Computer name** (up to 15 characters) then click **OK**.

2.4 Working on a network

A-Sharing a folder with network users

From your computer, you can access shared folders on other workstations on the network. So that another network user can access your documents too, you should share the folder which contains them. To share a folder, you need an adequate level of permissions.

▓ Right-click the folder or the disk drive concerned then take the **Sharing** option.

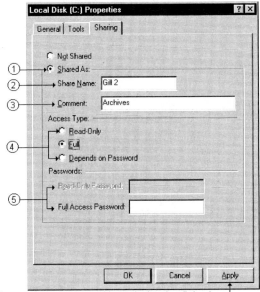

click to apply the settings without closing the dialog box⌐

① Activate this option.

② If necessary, change the share name for the folder. This is the name that will be seen on other workstations when they access your computer.

③ Enter a comment, if required.

④ Specify what type of access is allowed.

⑤ If required, give a password for **Read-Only** and/or **Full** access.

⇨ *To unshare a folder, right-click it, choose the **Sharing** option then activate the **Not Shared** option and click **OK**.*

⇨ *The **Sharing** option can only appear if file sharing has been enabled in the properties of your network (go to **My Network Places** and right-click; choose the **Properties** option and set the **File and Print Sharing** options).*

B-Using My Network Places

My Network Places shows all the workstations, printers and other shared resources on the network to which you are connected.

▓ Double-click the **My Network Places** icon on the desktop or from the Explorer, double-click **My Network Places**.

▓ To access all the workstations, double-click **Entire Network** or if the **Folders** explorer bar is showing, click the + sign that precedes **Entire Network**.

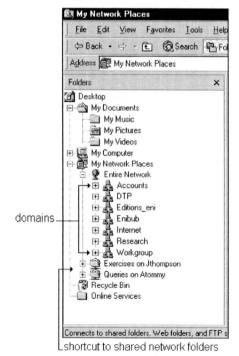

domains

shortcut to shared network folders

Access the domain (if there are several), the workstation then the shared folder, either by successive double-clicks or by expanding the branch in question.

C-Creating a shortcut to a network folder in the Explorer

Double-click the **Add Network Place** icon in the **My Network Places** window.

Use the **Type the location of the Network Place** box to specify the location of the shared network folder you wish to access or click the **Browse** button to look for it.

Click **Next**.

Give a name for the shortcut to the shared folder (this name appears in the **My Network Places** list) then click the **Finish** button.

⇨ *To go to the contents of this folder again, simply click the shortcut name in the file hierarchy, from the Explorer window.*

D-Mapping a drive letter to a workstation

Make sure you are in the Explorer window.

Tools - Map Network Drive

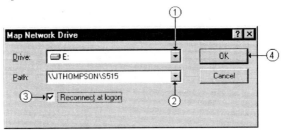

① Select the letter you wish to assign to the computer in question.

② Give the complete path to the network folder.

③ Make sure this option is active if you want the connection to be re-established automatically at the start of every Windows Millennium session.

④ Click to confirm.

⇨ *To disassociate the drive letter from the workstation, use Tools - Disconnect Network Drive.*

E-Finding a computer on the network

From the desktop, double-click the **My Network Places** icon then click the **Search** button.

If necessary, click the **Computers** link in the left pane.

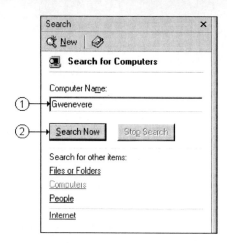

① Give the name of the computer you are looking for.

② Click to start the search.

When the search is finished, the result appears in the right side of the screen.

F- Modifying a logon password

Passwords allow you to protect your work, providing they are difficult to crack. There are some elementary rules you should follow to create an effective password: mix letters and numbers, do not use you own name or surname or those of friends and family and avoid using names of people or objects. The ideal password is an invented string of characters.

Windows Millennium accepts passwords of up to 127 characters (Windows 95 or 98 only accept 14). If you work in a network with computers using Windows 95 or 98, avoid passwords of more than 14 characters if you wish to log on from another computer.

▓ To change the logon password, click the **Start** button then activate the **Settings** menu and choose the **Control Panel** option.

▓ Double-click the **Passwords** icon.

▓ Click the **Change Windows Password** button on the **Change Passwords** page.

▓ If necessary, activate any other passwords that need to be modified.

▓ Click **OK**.

▓ Give your **Old password**, the **New password** then type the new password again into the **Confirm new password** box and click **OK** twice.

3.1 Files in Windows applications

A-Creating a new file

▓ **File**   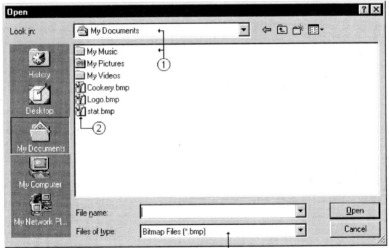   Ctrl **N**
New

▓ If you need to, save any changes in the active file.

⇨ *Many applications use document windows and can manage several open files at once.*

B-Opening a file

▓ **File**   Ctrl **O**
Open

▓ If necessary, save the changes to the active file.

the extension depends on the type of file ⅃

① Select the drive containing the file and then double-click to open its folder.

② Double-click the name of the file.

⇨ *To close a file, simply close its document window by clicking the* ✕ *button at the top of the window.*

⇨ *In some applications, the* **File** *menu gives you access to the last four files opened.*

⇨ *The* **Documents** *menu in the* **Start** *menu gives you access to the last fifteen files modified in Windows.*

Windows Millennium Edition

APPLICATIONS

C-Saving a file

A new file

File
Save

Ctrl S

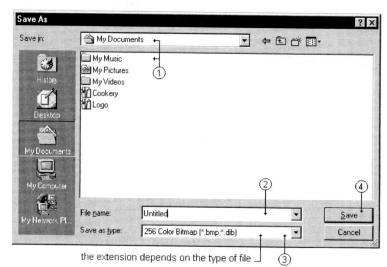

the extension depends on the type of file ⏗

① Tell Windows in which folder to save the document.

② Enter the name you want to give the new document: you can use up to 255 characters (upper- and lower case), but you cannot use \ / : " ? * < > and |.

③ Select a format for the document.

④ Click to save.

*The file name appears on the title bar. If the **Hide file extensions for known file types** option (in **Tools - Folder Options - View** tab) is deactivated, the file name is followed by a three-character extension, which is linked to the file format (for example, text files generally carry a TXT extension, Excel workbooks have a XLS extension, Word documents have a DOC extension, etc).*

An existing file

File
Save

Ctrl S

Saving goes ahead without further confirmation.

⇨ *To save a document under a different name, use the **File - Save As** command.*

D-Using the Open and Save As dialog boxes

Go to the **Open** dialog box with **File - Open** or to the **Save As** dialog box with **File - Save** or **Save As.**

Selecting a drive/folder

use to go the last folder visited

list of existing folders within the selected drive or folder

use to go to the folder above

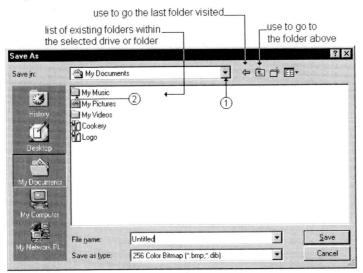

① To specify where a file you wish to open is located or where to save a file, open the **Look in** or **Save in** list and select the drive and/or folder concerned. You can also click one of the shortcuts offered in the **Places Bar**.

② Go to the folder concerned by double-clicking the folder icon.

You will see any subfolders it contains plus a list of the files within the active folder.

Creating a folder

use to modify the file list view

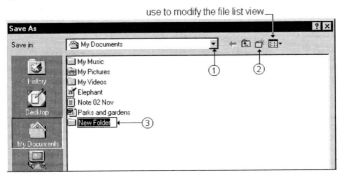

① Go to the drive or folder in which you wish to create a new folder.

Windows Millennium Edition

② Click to create a new folder.

③ Enter a name for your new folder then press Enter .

⇨ *To delete a folder or file in the **Open** or **Save As** dialog box, click its name then press the Del key. Confirm deletion by clicking **Yes**.*

E-Undoing your last action

In most Windows applications, it is possible to undo your last action.

▦ **Edit** Ctrl **Z**
   Undo

⇨ *In some applications, for instance Paint, you can undo several of your last actions.*

⇨ *The tool button and shortcut key are not necessarily available in every application.*

F-Printing a document

▦ **File - Print** or Ctrl **P**

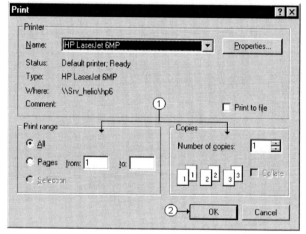

① Specify the printing options.

② Click this button.

⇨ *You can also print without going through the **Print** dialog box by clicking the ⎙ tool button.*

G-Managing the print queue

▦ **Start - Settings - Printers**

▦ Double-click the printer you wish to use.

- To interrupt the printing of a document, right-click the file name then activate the **Pause Printing** option. To resume printing of the selected file, right-click the file name and deactivate **Pause Printing** option.

  The other files in the queue "overtake" the paused document.

- To cancel the printing of a document altogether, right-click the document and choose **Cancel Printing**. To cancel the printing of several documents, select them with ⇧ Shift -clicks or Ctrl -clicks then right-click the selection and choose **Cancel Printing**.

3.2 Copying, linking and embedding

A - Copying/moving data

*Data can be copied and moved via the **Clipboard**: this is a part of the memory that Windows reserves for the transfer of data (text, images, sounds etc) within a file or from one file to another.*

- Select the text to transfer.
- To copy the data, use:

  Edit   **C**
  Copy

- To move then use:

  Edit   Ctrl **X**
  Cut

  *The data are transferred to the Windows' clipboard. If you have used the **Cut** command, they are no longer visible.*

- Put the insertion point where you want the data in the clipboard to appear.

  This can be somewhere in another file, even a file in a different application.

- Copy the contents of the clipboard using the command:

  Edit   **V**
  Paste

  The data are still in the clipboard: you can paste them as many times, in as many places, as you want.

⇨ *The content of the clipboard changes when you copy in new data. It is cleared when you turn off your computer.*

⇨ *You can view the contents of the clipboard: click the **Start** button and point to the **Programs** option. Next, point to the **Accessories** menu and then the **System Tools** option. Click the **Clipboard Viewer** option.*

⇨ *When you work in Office 2000 applications, copied or moved data is placed in the Office Clipboard, which is able to store several items simultaneously.*

Windows Millennium Edition

B-Inserting an entire file into another file

By the techniques of Object Linking and Embedding, also known as OLE, Windows optimises the transfer of data from one application to another:

- **Embedding**: *the embedded object is an integral part of its destination file (the size of this file increases in consequence).*
- **Linking**: *the destination file does not contain the object transferred: it contains a linking formula indicating where the object can be found when the application needs it (to display or print).*

Here are the definitions of three terms you will meet in the following pages.

- *An **object** is any item that you create in any application (it can be a table or a chart from a spreadsheet, a picture from a bitmap application, a sound or an image from a multimedia application...).*
- *Only **server** applications can produce objects which may be inserted into other applications (Paint, Sound Recorder and the spreadsheet Microsoft Excel function as server applications).*
- *Only **client** applications are able to accept the insertion of an object (WordPad and the word processor Microsoft Word function as client applications). Some applications can be both server and client.*

Inserting an existing file

Start in the client application, open the destination document, then go to the place where you wish to insert the document.

Insert - Object

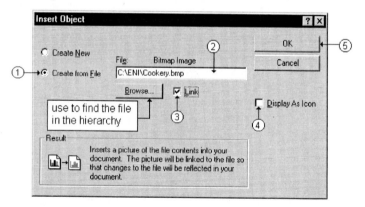

① Activate this option.

② Give the name of the file you wish to insert.

③ Activate this option if the object is to be linked, not embedded.

④ Activate this option if you want an icon to represent the source file in the client application.

⑤ Click to insert the object.

⇨ *If you have established a link, the image of the object in the client application file will be updated automatically when changes are made to the original in the server application (providing that the **Update** option is set to **Automatic** in **Edit - Links**). If the client application is loaded in memory, the file is updated at once; if it is inactive, Windows offers to update the file the next time you open it.*

⇨ *Double-click the inserted file and you start the server application.*

Inserting a new file

▓ In the client application, go to the place where you want to insert the object.

▓ **Insert - Object**

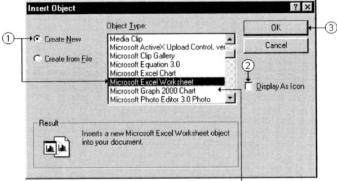

this list depends on the server applications ⌐
installed on your disk

① Check that this option is active, then select the type of object you wish to insert. This is determined by the application in which you are going to create it.

② Activate this option if you want an icon to represent the object in the destination file.

③ Click to insert the object.

The server application window replaces the client application window; this is in-place editing: the client application document is still visible, but the menus and toolbars of the client application window have been temporarily replaced so that you can create the object. This technique is only available for applications which support OLE 2.0. For the others, the server application appears in a separate window overlapping the client application window.

▓ Create the object with the tools and options of the server application.

- To return to the client application:
  - if the server application appears in a separate window, close it, then click **Yes** to update the client application file,
  - if you are working in-place, click anywhere in the window outside the embedded object.

C-Managing a link with an external object

- Once in the destination file, use the command:
  Edit - Links

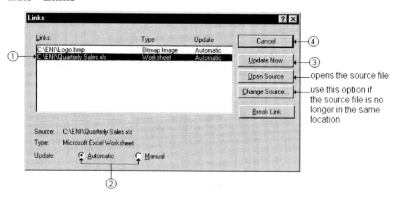

① Select the link that interests you, by clicking it in the list.

② Choose to have Windows update the link automatically, or to do it manually.

③ If you have chosen **Manual**, click this button to update the object in the destination file.

④ Close the dialog box.

⇨ *You can also manage a link in the **Link** page of the dialog box dealing with the object's properties. To open this dialog box, select the object then go into **Edit - Object Properties** or* Alt Enter *or right-click the object and choose **Object Properties**.*

D-Modifying an embedded object

▨ To edit the embedded object in place, double-click it, or right-click and choose **(type of) Object** then **Edit**. To open the server application in a separate window, click the object with the right mouse button, choose **(type of) Object** then **Open**.

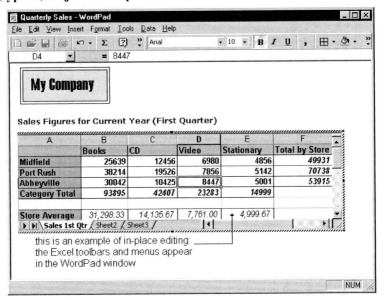

▨ Make the changes you require.

▨ Close the server application window, or if you are editing in place, click in the document outside the object to activate the client application.

E-Copying an external object into a document

You can also use the clipboard to copy and insert an object into a document.

▨ From inside the server application, copy the data into the clipboard.

▨ Go into the client application and to the place where you wish to copy the object.

▨ **Edit - Paste Special**

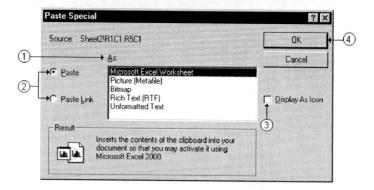

① Select the format you require for the pasted object.

② If you intend to embed the object, activate the **Paste** option, or activate the **Paste Link** option to establish a link with the source file.

③ Activate this option if you wish to represent the object with an icon.

④ Click to paste the object.

F-Displaying an inserted object as an icon

- Click to select the object.
- **Edit - Object Properties** or ⟦Alt⟧⟦Enter⟧
- Click the **View** tab then activate the **Display as icon** option.
- If you are not happy with the icon proposed, click **Change Icon**.
- Click **OK** to close the dialog box.
- To see the object's contents, double-click its icon.

G-Capturing a screen

You have the possibility of capturing the elements that you see on your screen at a given time and making an image from it.

- Make sure the screen shows just what you wish to capture.
- Press the ⟦Prt Sc⟧ key to capture the entire screen or ⟦Alt⟧ ⟦Prt Sc⟧ to capture only the active window (an open dialog box for example).

The screen capture is copied into the Windows clipboard.

- Go into the Paint application and if necessary, create a new document.
- Insert the contents of the clipboard using **Edit - Paste** or ⟦Ctrl⟧ **V**.
- Save the Paint document if you wish to keep your screen capture.

3.3 The Paint application

A-The Paint window

Apart from the items common to all Windows applications, the Paint window contains the following:

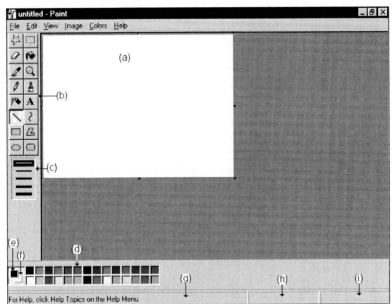

(a) The **image area** is the space where you work.

(b) The **tool box** contains the tools which will help you create and manage your pictures.

(c) The **option box** can contain options corresponding to the selected tool.

(d) The **colour box** contains a choice of colours for the foreground (e) and background (f). The selected colours are displayed to the left of the box.

(g) The **status bar** contains a help message display, an indicator of the pointer's position in the image area (h) and an indicator of the current drawing's dimensions (i).

➪ *The tool box and colour box can be moved by dragging them.*

➪ *For the tool box, colour box and status bar to be visible, the corresponding options in the View menu must be active.*

➪ *It is possible to hide the Paint window and show only the image it contains: use View - View Bitmap or* Ctrl *F.*

B-Resizing the image area

■ Point to one of the handles on the drawing area: point to one of the corner handles if you wish to modify the height and the width simultaneously.

■ Drag the handle.

As you drag, the changing dimensions can be seen on the status bar.

⇨ *If you enlarge the image area, the added space appears in the background colour currently selected.*

■ **Image - Attributes** or Ctrl **E**

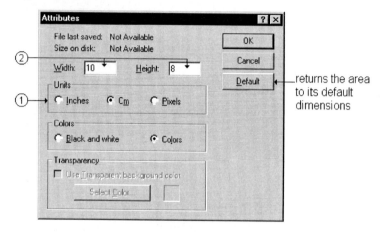

returns the area to its default dimensions

① Choose one of the measurement units offered.

② Give the width and height of the image area, in the selected unit.

⇨ *You can carry out this action even if there is already a picture in the image area. If you reduce the size of the image area, you will lose any parts of the drawing that fall outside the new limits.*

⇨ *When increasing the size of the image area, check that the new size, combined with the existing printing margins, is not larger than the size of the paper used for printing.*

C-Zooming in on an image

■ Select the 🔍 tool.

The mouse pointer appears as a rectangle.

■ Move the pointer over the area you wish to magnify then click.

■ If necessary, show a miniature of the image (a thumbnail) with **View - Zoom - Show Thumbnail**.

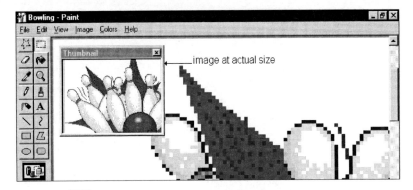

image at actual size

▦ Click the 🔍 tool again: the active zoom level can be seen in the options box.

When you click in the image area with the 🔍 *tool, Paint automatically applies the last zoom level used.*

▦ To return to the original magnification, click the **1x** option.

⬡▦ Use the following shortcut keys:

Ctrl Pg Dn to apply the maximum zoom value.

Ctrl Pg Up to return to actual size.

▦ **View - Zoom - Custom**

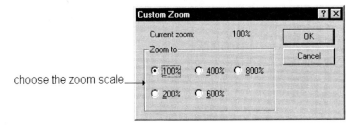

choose the zoom scale

D-Working in zoom view

▦ To show the grid when you are in zoom view, use the command:

View - Zoom - Show Grid or Ctrl **G**

▦ Select a tool depending on the changes you wish to make.

▦ Modify the image as if you were in normal view. To insert new dots, use

the ✏ tool: point to the appropriate square in the grid and click with the left mouse button to insert a dot of the foreground colour, or with the right mouse button to insert a dot of the background colour.

APPLICATIONS

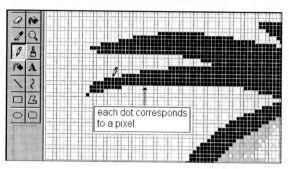

each dot corresponds to a pixel

⇨ *In zoom view, you can insert a series of dots forming a straight line by holding down* ⌠⇧ Shift⌡ *and dragging.*

E-Wallpapering the desktop

The picture used as the desktop background (wallpaper) is defined in the desktop properties, but you can also apply wallpaper in Paint.

▓ Open the document containing the image you want to use.

▓ Depending on how you want to arrange the image on the desktop (repeated picture or central picture), select one of the options from the **File** menu: **Set As Wallpaper (Tiled)** or **Set As Wallpaper (Centered)**.

F-Creating a drawing

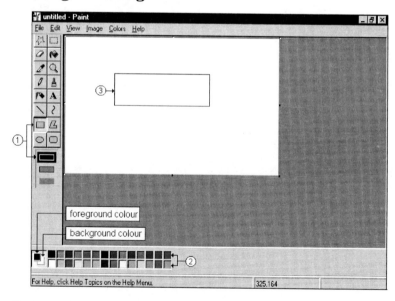

foreground colour

background colour

① Select the tool which corresponds to what you want to draw. If there are options connected with the tool, choose one of the options.

② Select the colours: left-click to select the foreground colour and right-click to select the background colour.

③ Drag to draw: use the left mouse button to draw in the foreground colour and the right mouse button to draw in the background colour.

⇨ *Background colour is only used on figures with fill colour or when erasing drawing objects.*

G-Drawing a shape

Drawing a rectangle (or square)/an ellipse (or circle)

▓ Select one of the following tools:

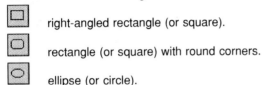

right-angled rectangle (or square).

rectangle (or square) with round corners.

ellipse (or circle).

▓ Select the type of shape to draw.

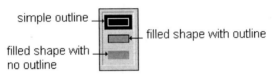

simple outline

filled shape with outline

filled shape with no outline

▓ Select your colours then drag to draw the shape.

▓ If you want to draw a perfect square or circle, hold the [⇧ Shift] key down while you are dragging.

Drawing a straight line

▓ Click ◤.

▓. In the options box, determine the thickness of the line.

▓ Select the foreground colour then drag to draw the line.

▓ To draw an absolutely straight horizontal or vertical line, or an oblique line at 45°, hold [⇧ Shift] down while you are drawing and only release it after you have released the mouse button.

Drawing a curve

▓ Select the [?] tool.

▓ Determine the thickness of the line in the options box.

▓ Select just a foreground colour.

▓ Position the pointer then drag to draw a line linking the two ends of the curve.

▓ Click the line you have drawn and drag it upwards or downwards to make it curve.

Windows Millennium Edition

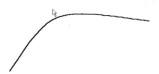

▨ Click again and drag in the opposite direction to make a second curve.

⇨ *Once the original line is drawn, you only have two opportunities to click and modify the curve. If you click a third time, Windows guesses that you want to draw another curved line.*

⇨ *Until you release the left mouse button a second time, you can erase the curve by clicking with the right mouse button.*

Drawing a triangle/a polygon

▨ Select the ▦ tool.

▨ In the options box, select the type of polygon you wish to draw then choose your drawing colours.

▨ Drag the mouse to draw the first side of the polygon.

▨ To draw a triangle, double-click the place where you want to put the third corner to close the triangle.

▨ To draw a polygon, click at each corner and to close the shape, double-click when you reach the final corner.

⇨ *When drawing a polygon, right-click to draw with the background colour.*

H-Managing text

▨ Select the **A** tool.

▨ If you want the background of your text box to be in the background colour currently active, take option (a). If you do not want the text box to have any colour of its own, take option (b).

▨ Select the colour of the text (foreground colour), and change the background colour, if necessary, for an opaque text box.

▨ Click the place where the text should appear, or drag to draw the text box.

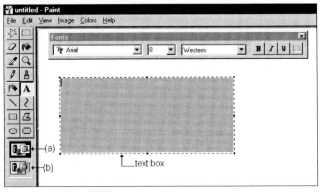

(a)

(b)

text box

- Type in the text. Press [Enter] to change line.

  As long as the insertion point is flashing in the text box, you can press [Esc] to cancel the text and close the text toolbar.

- While you are still typing, as long as you have not clicked outside the text, you can use the [⬅] key to delete.

  If you have already clicked elsewhere in the window, this key is no longer available, and only the eraser tool can delete the text, since it has been incorporated into the image.

- While you are still typing, providing that you have not clicked outside the text, you can use the options in the toolbar to alter your text presentation.

- Once you have finished entering and formatting text, click in the window outside the text box.

  This gives your text the status of an image: you can no longer intervene to modify its content or formatting.

  ⇨ *You can resize the text box by dragging one of its handles.*

I- Erasing a drawing

- Select the [⬜] tool.
- Select the size of the eraser in the options box.
- Select the same background colour as the image area.
- Drag along the lines you want to erase.

  When you erase a drawing, you paint over it with the background colour. Whatever its original colour, the drawing disappears.

  ⇨ *You can, of course, retrieve the drawing by **Edit - Undo**.*

  ⇨ *To erase part of an image, you can select it by means of [⬚] or [⬚], then press [Del].*

  ⇨ *To erase the whole image, activate **Image - Clear Image** or [Ctrl][⇧ Shift] **N**; you can also create a new document (**File - New**).*

J- Selecting part of the image

▒ If the part of the image you wish to select can be enclosed in a rectangle, choose the ▢ tool. If it is irregular, choose .

▒ If you want the uncoloured areas of the selection to remain colourless when the selection is transferred onto a coloured background, take option (a) (opaque selection). If you intend these areas to adopt the colour of their destination, take option (b) (transparent selection).

(a)—▶
(b)—▶

▒ Drag to enclose the area you are selecting.

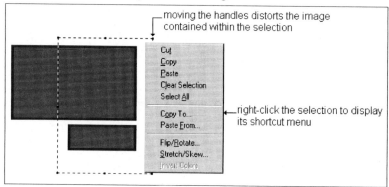

▒ To cancel the selection, click anywhere outside it or press Esc.

K-Moving a drawing

▒ Select the drawing.

▒ Check that the active background colour corresponds to the background colour of the selection.

▒ Position the pointer inside the dotted selection border.

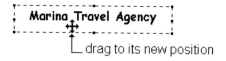

⇨ *You can send the drawing back to its original place by* **Edit - Undo**.

L-Copying a drawing

Copying inside the picture area

▓ Select the drawing.

▓ Select the first option in the options box to make an opaque copy, or the second option to make a transparent one.

▓ Move the pointer inside the selection.

▓ Hold down Ctrl and drag to copy the drawing.

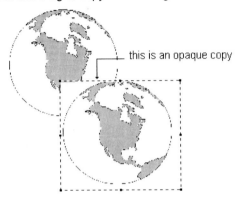

this is an opaque copy

⇨ *If you hold the* ⇧ Shift *key down, instead of the* Ctrl *key, you create a multiple copy effect:*

Copying into a new file

▓ Select the image/part of an image you wish to copy.

▓ **Edit - Copy To**

▓ Select the folder, and enter the name of the destination document.

▓ Click **Save**.

Copying from another file

▓ In the destination file, use **Edit - Paste From**.

▓ Open the folder containing the source file, and double-click its name.

▓ In the options box, choose between an opaque or a transparent copy.

▓ Once the image is in the Paint window, drag it to its place.

▓ Cancel the selection by clicking outside it.

M-Resizing/skewing an image

To resize an image, start by selecting it then point to one of the selection handles.

drag here to resize
the image

⇨ *The disadvantage of this technique is that it does not guarantee the proportions of the image.*

Select the image.

Image - Stretch/Skew or Ctrl **W**

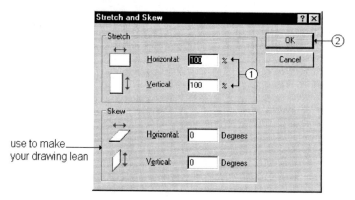

① Select the **Horizontal** option to modify the width of the image and/or the **Vertical** option to modify its height, then specify the percentage of enlargement/reduction you wish to see.

② Click to confirm.

N-Rotating an image

Select the image and activate opaque/transparent selection.

Image - Flip/Rotate or Ctrl **R**

Select one of the options:

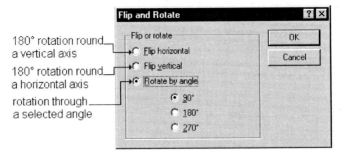

180° rotation round a vertical axis

180° rotation round a horizontal axis

rotation through a selected angle

Flip and Rotate

Flip or rotate
- ○ Flip horizontal
- ○ Flip vertical
- ● Rotate by angle
  - ● 90°
  - ○ 180°
  - ○ 270°

OK
Cancel

⇨ *If you do not start by making a selection, the effect will apply to the entire image area.*

O-Managing colours

Painting an area

▓ Activate the colour in the colour box.

▓ Select the 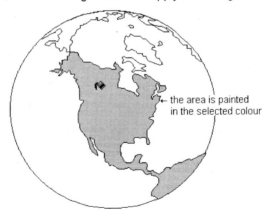 tool.

▓ Position the pointer so that it is pouring paint onto the area you want to colour.

▓ If you want to paint the area in the foreground colour, click with the left button, and click with the right button to apply the background colour.

← the area is painted in the selected colour

⇨ *You can undo the action by **Edit - Undo**.*

⇨ *The same tool can be used to change the colour of a line.*

⇨ *If the area you are painting is not closed, the paint will run into adjacent areas.*

APPLICATIONS

Creating a custom colour

▨ In the colour box, click the colour you wish to replace with your custom colour.

▨ **Colors - Edit Colors**

▨ If you wish, select a base colour that you wish to modify to create a custom colour then click the **Define Custom Colors** button.

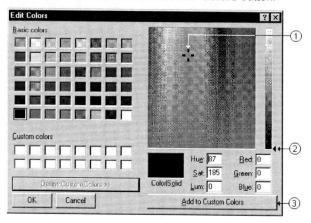

① Click the required colour.

② Move the luminosity slider up or down to define the colour's brightness.

③ Click to add the colour to the **Custom colors** palette.

Copying colour from one area of the image to another

▨ Click the ![tool] tool button in the toolbox.

▨ Click the area whose colour you wish to copy: left-click to copy the colour as the foreground colour or right-click to copy it as the background colour.

The current foreground (or background) colour is replaced by the colour you chose.

▨ Click the ![tool] tool button in the toolbox.

▨ Click the area you wish to paint with the copied colour.

Replacing a colour by erasing

▨ As your foreground colour, select the colour you want to erase.

▨ Select the colour which should replace it as background colour.

▨ Select the ![tool] tool.

▨ Hold down the right mouse button and drag over the colour you wish to erase.

3.4 The Windows Movie Maker application

A-The Windows Movie Maker window

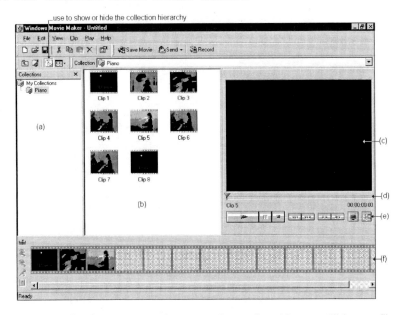

(a) **collections** are used to store the audio, video or still image files that you record or import.

(b) these are the **clips** contained in the selected collection

(c) the **monitor** is used to view the selected clip or an entire movie.

(d) the cursor on the **seek bar** moves when an audio or video file is playing in the preview screen.

(e) the **navigation buttons** allow you to browse through a clip or movie.

(f) the **workspace** is the area in which you construct and edit your movies before saving them as an image file. You can use either a **Storyboard** or **Timeline** view, by activating the corresponding option in the **View** menu. When in **Timeline** view, the workspace displays two bars: the first holds the still pictures and video clips and the second (the audio bar) holds the sound clips.

B-Recording video or audio source material

You must record any audio/video source material into Windows Movie Maker for it to be converted to digital format. The source material will appear in the form of clips which can then be integrated into your projects. Source material can be obtained from a variety of capture devices, such as an analogue or digital video camera, a Web camera or a microphone.

File
Record

Ctrl R

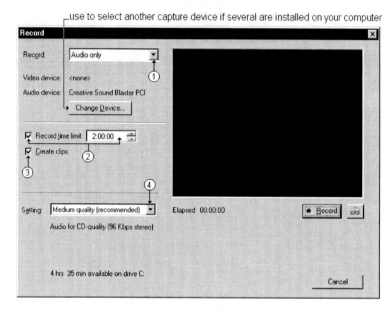

①Select the option that corresponds to the type of material you wish to record.

②Tick this option then enter a value in the text box if you want the recording to stop automatically after a certain time.

③Tick this option to instruct Movie Maker to create clips.

④Select the required quality setting.

Using the commands on your video recorder or analogue video camera, find the source material you wish to record.

Click the **Record** button.

Use the commands on your video recorder or analogue video camera to play the material: the video should appear on the monitor.

Click the **Stop** button to stop recording manually. If you do not stop it manually, recording will continue until the **Record time limit** has elapsed.

- Select the drive then the folder in which you want to save the file, enter the **File name** then click **Save**.

  A new collection containing the clips from the recorded source material appears in the list of collections: the clips can be seen in the right pane.

- Stop the tape using the commands on your recorder or camera.

C-Recording a narration

A narration is an sound file created to accompany a movie (to comment on the clips shown for example).

- Go into **Timeline** view (**View - Timeline** or click 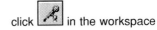).
- Open the project in which you want to use the narration.
- **File**
  Record Narration   click 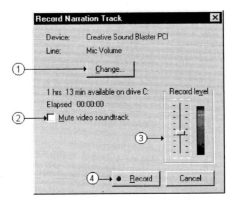 in the workspace

① If the capture device and/or input line are not those indicated at the top of the dialog box, click this button to make another choice.

② Tick this option if your project contains a video clip with audio content and you do not wish to hear the audio soundtrack of that clip.

③ Increase or decrease the volume of the narration.

④ Click to start recording the narration.

While the narration is recording, the video project plays in the monitor.

- When you have finished, click **Stop**.
- Select the drive then the folder in which you want to save the file, enter the **File name** then click **Save**.

  The narration is recorded as an audio file (.wav). It is inserted automatically as an audio clip at the beginning of the project's audio bar in the workspace, as well as in the current collection.

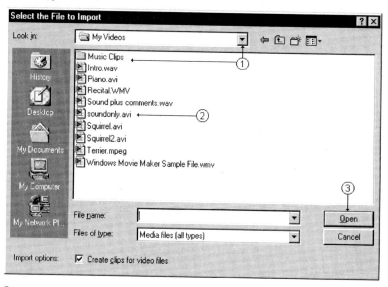

If you wish, move the audio clip to another position on the audio bar, for example, beneath the video or still clips that require a commentary.

D-Importing a file

You can import audio files (such as .mp3, .asf, .wma), video files (such as .wmv, .asf, .avi, .mpg) or still images (.jpg, .gif and so on) into Windows Movie Maker. If you import a still image, for example, to create a title slide, it must be in bitmap format and it should measure 320 pixels by 240 pixels.

▨ Click the collection into which you want to import the project.

▨ **File - Import** or `Ctrl` I

① Select the drive then the folder where the file you are importing is stored.

② Select the file you wish to import. To import several files at once, use `⇧ Shift`-clicks to select adjacent objects or `Ctrl`-clicks to select nonadjacent objects.

③ Click to import the file.

*If you import an audio file or still images, the new clips appear in the currently selected collection. If you import a video file, Windows Movie Maker displays the clips in a new collection, which, by default, takes the name of the imported file. This new collection is created in the **My Collections** folder.*

Next, save this file like any other Windows file **File - Save** or 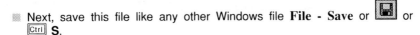 or `Ctrl` **S**.

⇨ *Project files carry a MSWMM extension.*

⇨ *To open or create a project, you can use the **Open** and **New** commands in the **File** menu.*

⇨ *Even after you have recorded it in Windows Movie Maker, the source file stays in its original place. Clips are not physically stored in the collections area; what exists is a linking formula that refers back to the source file. If you try to work with clips whose source file has been moved, deleted or renamed, Windows Movie Maker will display a message asking if you want to search for the source file. If the file has simply been moved, click **Yes** to look for the file with the **Browse for** dialog box; if the file has been deleted or renamed, it cannot be recovered in this way, so click **No**.*

E-Modifying a clip's properties

Click the collection concerned then click the required clip.

View - Properties or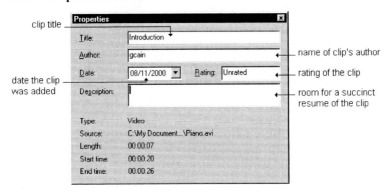

⇨ *You can only modify the properties of clips in the collections area, not those that figure in the workspace. In addition to this, if you add a clip to the workspace then modify its properties in the collections area, the clip inserted in the workspace will still display its old properties.*

F-Creating a collection

Click the collection into which you want to add the new one.

*You can also select a collection by opening the **Collection** drop-down list on the **Location** toolbar then clicking the name of the collection to select it.*

File - New - Collection or

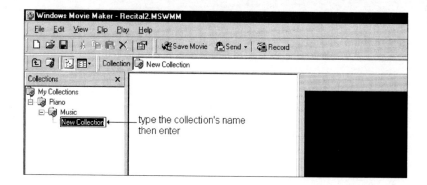

type the collection's name
then enter

G-Managing clips/collections

░ To modify clip display, choose one of the options from the **View** menu:

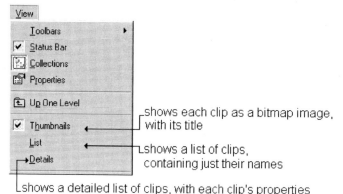

shows each clip as a bitmap image, with its title

shows a list of clips, containing just their names

shows a detailed list of clips, with each clip's properties

The selected view is applied to all the clips in the collection.

The same options can be found in the drop-down list on the *tool button, on the Collections toolbar.*

░ To move the selected collection, drag it to its new location.

░ To copy or move clips, select them then drag them to the new position. If you are copying, hold down the `Ctrl` key as you drag.

░ To rename a clip or a collection, select the clip or collection in question, click its name once again or activate the **Edit - Rename** command. Type the new name then press `Enter`.

You cannot rename the clips contained in the workspace, only the clips visible in the collections area can be renamed. If you add a clip to the workspace then change its name in the collections area, the property sheet of the inserted clip will still display its former name.

░ To delete clips or a collection, select the clips or collection then use:

Edit
Delete

▦ Click **Yes** to confirm the deletion.

⇨ *You can also use the **Edit - Delete** command or* ☒ *or* ⌊Del⌋ *to delete selected clips from the workspace.*

H-Adding one or more clips to a project

▤ ▦ Go into **Timeline** view (**View - Timeline** or click 🔲).

▦ Click the collection concerned then select the clips you wish to add to the project.

▦ **Clip - Add To Storyboard**

⇨ *Video clips and still images are visible on the first bar in the workspace while audio clips appear on the second bar (the **audio bar**).*

🖰 ▦ Go into **Timeline** view (**View - Timeline** or click 🔲).

▦ Click the collection concerned then select the clips you wish to add to the project.

▦ Drag the selection onto the first bar of the workspace (if you are adding video or still images) or onto the second bar (if you are adding audio clips).

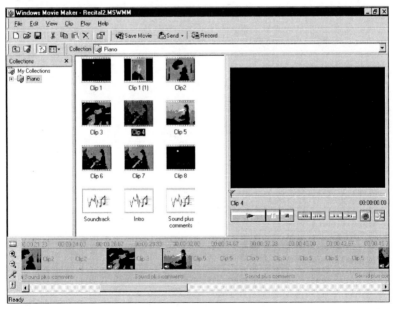

▦ Release the mouse button when a blue vertical line appears in the position where you wish to add the clips in the project (this can be before or after a clip or between two clips).

⇨ *If you try to insert an audio clip into a project but you are not in **Timeline** view, Windows Movie Maker will display a message telling you that an audio clip cannot be added to the storyboard and asking if you would like it to switch to a timeline view so you can insert the selected clip(s).*

⇨ *The* ⊖ *and* ⊕ *buttons that appear in the workspace can be used to zoom in or out of the clips contained in the project.*

I- Trimming a clip

If you only want to use part of a clip in your project, you can trim away the rest. Trimming simply removes the beginning or the end of the clip within the project, it has no effect on the clip's source material.

▨ In the workspace, click the clip concerned.

The clip appears on the monitor.

▨ To trim the beginning of a clip, point to the slider on the monitor's seek bar, drag it to the end of the section you wish to remove then use the **Clip - Set Start Trim Point** command. The material from the start of the clip up to the slider position is trimmed off.

▨ To trim the end off a clip, point to the slider on the monitor's seek bar, drag it to the start of the section you wish to remove then use the **Clip - Set End Trim Point** command. The material from the slider's position up to the end of the clip is trimmed off.

⇨ *You can also trim a clip by selecting it in the workspace then dragging the start trim marker and/or the end trim marker:*

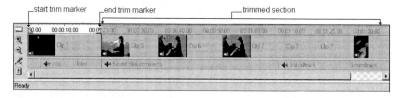

⇨ *You can cancel all the trim points on a clip. To do this, select the clip then use the **Clip - Clear Trim Points** command.*

J- Splitting a clip

You may want to split a video or audio clip in two, perhaps to insert another clip in the middle (audio, video or still image) or to create a transition.

▨ In the workspace or in the collections area, select the clip you wish to split.

▨ Point to the slider on the seek bar then drag it to the position where you wish to split the clip.

▨ **Clip**
  Split (beneath the monitor)

Ctrl ⇧ Shift S

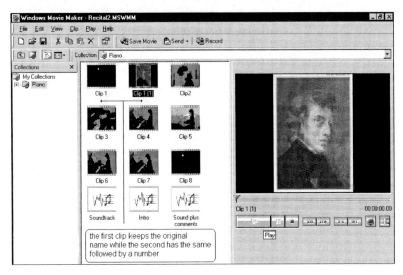

the first clip keeps the original name while the second has the same followed by a number

⇨ *If you split a clip in the workspace, the clip in the collections area remains intact and vice versa.*

⇨ *To combine two or more adjacent clips, select them in the workspace or the collections area then use the* **Clip - Combine** *command or* `Ctrl` `⇧ Shift` *C: the new clip takes the name and properties of the first clip in the selected group.*

K-Creating a transition

A transition is a visual effect applied when one clip (video or still image) replaces another during the movie. When a transition is applied between two clips, the last frames of the first clip disappear gradually while the first frames of the next clip appear.

Go into **Timeline** view (**View - Timeline** or click ⊞).

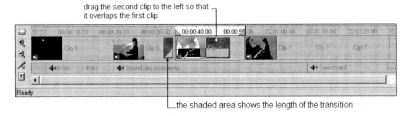

drag the second clip to the left so that it overlaps the first clip

the shaded area shows the length of the transition

⇨ *To change the length of a transition, select the clip on the right of the transition you wish to modify and drag it towards the left to increase the length of the transition or to the right to decrease it.*

⇨ *To delete a transition, click the clip on the right of the transition you wish to delete and drag it towards the right until the transition area disappears.*

⇨ *You can apply the same technique to two audio clips if you wish them to play simultaneously.*

⇨ *To modify the balance, use the* **Edit - Audio Levels** *command or click* ⬛ *in the workspace. To increase the volume level of an audio clip, drag the slider to the right. To increase the volume of a video clip, drag the slider to the left.*

L-Previewing a clip/project

▨ Select the collection or open the project containing the clip(s) you wish to preview.

▨ To preview one or more clips, select them in the collections area or if they have been added to the project, select them in the workspace then use **Play - Play/Pause** or ⬛ or ⬛space⬛.

▨ To preview all the clips in a project, use **Play - Play Entire Storyboard/Timeline**.

▨ To stop the preview of one or more clips or an entire project, use **Play - Stop** or ⬛.

The monitor then automatically reverts to the first clip in the project seen in the workspace. If no project is open, the monitor will show nothing.

▨ To pause the preview, use **Play - Play/Pause** or ⬛.

▨ To preview one or more clips (or an entire project) full screen, use either **Play/Pause** or **Play Entire Storyboard/Timeline** in the **Play** menu to start playing then use **Play - Full Screen** or ⬛Alt⬛ ⬛Enter⬛ or ⬛. To close the full screen window, click inside it.

Click ⬛ *again to continue playing.*

⇨ *The* ⬛ *and* ⬛ *are used respectively to display the* **Previous Frame** *and the* **Next Frame** *of the clip shown on the monitor. The* ⬛ *and* ⬛ *buttons show the last clip* **Back** *or the next clip* **Forward** *in your project.*

M-Saving a movie in a file

When your project is complete, you can save it as a movie so you can view it on screen, send it with an e-mail or transfer it to a Web server.

▨ Create or open the project concerned.

▨ **File - Save Movie** or ⬛Ctrl⬛ **M**

You can also click the ⬛Save Movie⬛ *tool button.*

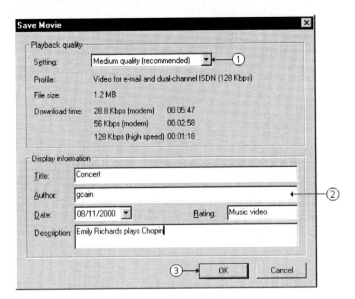

① Click the appropriate option for the required quality setting.

② Enter the information that should appear when the file is played.

③ Enter.

▓ Select the drive then the folder in which you wish to save your movie, enter the **File name** and click the **Save** button.

A message tells you that the movie has been saved and offers to play it for you.

▓ Click **Yes** to view your movie in the Windows Media Player or **No** to return to the Windows Movie Maker window.

▓ Once the movie has finished playing, click the ☒ button on the Windows Media Player window.

⇨ *A movie file carries a WMV extension.*

N-Sending a movie by e-mail

▓ Create or open the project concerned.

▓ **File - Send Movie To - E-mail**

▓ Open the **Setting** list and click the quality level required.

▓ In the **Display Information** frame, enter the information that should be displayed when the file is played then click **OK**.

▓ Type a **File name** for your movie then click **OK**.

▓ Select the e-mail application you wish to use to send your movie then click **OK**.

The e-mail application's new message window appears on the screen (depending on the application used, you may not see the same screen as below).

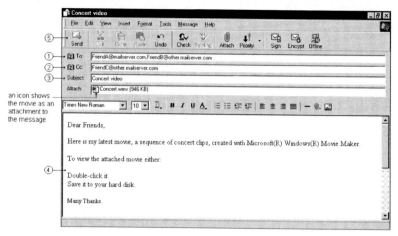

an icon shows the movie as an attachment to the message

① Enter the recipient's e-mail address or click the **To** button to choose it from the address book; if you are entering several addresses, separate them with semi-colons.

② Enter any recipients to whom you wish to send a carbon copy or select them by clicking **Cc**.

③ Enter the subject for your message.

④ Enter any text for your message; this area already contains text, which you can modify or delete.

⑤ Send the message.

▨ To view the movie in the Windows Media Player, the message recipient(s) should open the message then double-click the file icon.

⇨ *When you send a movie by e-mail, the movie files are saved by default in the C:\Windows\Temp folder.*

0-Transferring a movie to a Web server

You can place a movie on a Web server so it can be seen on an intranet or the Internet. Once you have placed the movie on the Web server, you must create a Web page containing a HTML link so that users only need to open the Web page and click the link to view the movie.

▨ Create or open the project concerned.

▨ **File - Send Movie To - Web Server**

▨ Open the **Setting** list then click the required quality setting.

▨ In the **Display Information** frame, enter the information that should be displayed when the file is played then click **OK**.

▨ Type a **File name** for your movie then click **OK**.

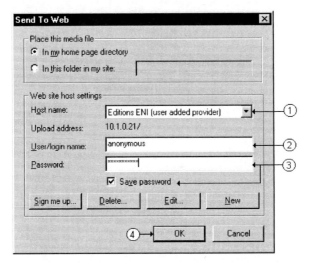

① Select the host profile you are using (this configuration gives the necessary settings for writing movies onto an FTP server and broadcasting them on a Web server).

② Enter your user name.

③ Enter your password then if necessary tick the **Save password** option.

④ Send your movie to the Web server.

The Sending To Web dialog box shows you how the transfer is progressing then asks you if you would like to visit the site.

▓ Click the **Visit Site Now** button to visit the Web site or close the dialog box.

▓ Next, create a Web page and insert in it a hyperlink that will take you to the movie file you have published on the Web.

▓ 3.5 Multimedia applications

A-Playing an audio CD

▓ Insert an audio CD into your CD-ROM drive then if necessary, start the **Windows Media Player** application.

title currently playing

Selecting a CD track to play

- If necessary, click **Now Playing**.
- Right-click the required track.
- Choose the **Play** option.
- Scroll through the track using the buttons on the **Windows Media Player**.

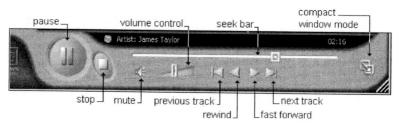

pause — volume control — seek bar — compact window mode

stop — mute — previous track — next track — rewind — fast forward

The track played appears in green in the window as does the playing time elapsed.

Downloading information from the Internet

It may occur that the first time you play a CD, the Windows Media Player does not recognise the album. In this case, Windows displays "unknown artist" for the CD. You can download information from the Internet about the CD currently in the CD-ROM drive.

- Click **CD Audio** then the **Get Names** button.
- Click the **Next** button.
- Give the name of the artist for your CD then click **Next**.

▓ In the list of artists found, select the name of your CD's artist then click **Next**.

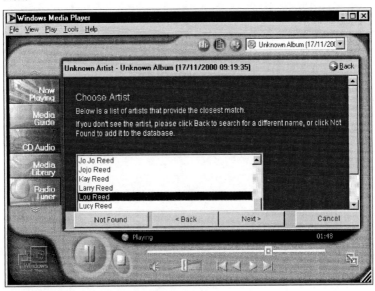

▓ Select the album then click **Next**.

▓ Click the **Finish** button to save the information found.

Defining what appears in the display area

You can modify the animated effect (or "visualization") that appears in the display area of the Now Playing page.

▓ Click **Now Playing**.

▓ Use **View - Visualizations**

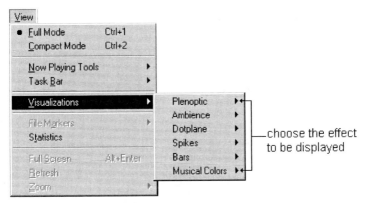

choose the effect
to be displayed

⇨ *You can also use the* ▣ *and* ▣ *buttons preceding the name of the animation effect.*

B-Watching a video

▓ **Start - Programs - Accessories - Entertainment - Windows Media Player**

You can also double-click a video file icon if you have one on your desktop.

▓ If you did not start the application from an existing file, use **File - Open** or Ctrl **O**.

If you want to open a file on the Internet, use File - Open URL and give the URL address.

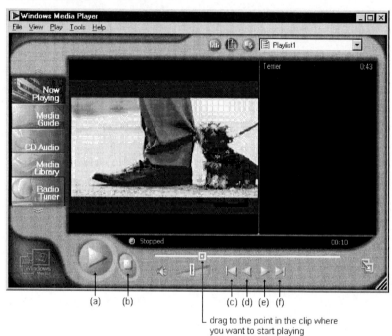

(a)   (b)   (c) (d) (e) (f)

drag to the point in the clip where you want to start playing

▓ Use the player command buttons to play the file:

(a)   Starts playing the file. The ▣ button pauses the currently playing file.

(b)   Stops the video.

(c)   When a file contains several clips, this button takes you back to the previous clip.

(d)   Rewinds the current clip (when there are several in the video). When you release the button, play resumes automatically.

(e)   When the file contains several clips, this button fast forwards the current clip: when you release it, play resumes automatically.

(f)   In a file containing several clips, this button goes forward to the start of the next clip.

C-Using the Sound Recorder

Playing a sound file

▓ Go into the **Sound Recorder** multimedia application.

▓ Open the .WAV sound file that you wish to listen to, using the **File - Open** command.

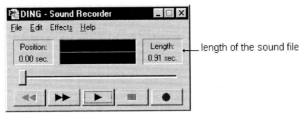

length of the sound file

▓ Click the ▶ button to play the sound file.

*You can raise or lower the volume by going into the **Volume Control** application or using the appropriate options in the **Effects** menu. In this same menu, you will find commands to increase or decrease the playing speed, to add echo or to reverse the order of play.*

Extracting part of a sound file

▓ Put the slider at the beginning of the part you want to extract.

▓ Go into **Edit** then **Delete Before Current Position**; click **OK** to confirm.

▓ Move the slider to the end of the part you want to keep.

▓ Go into **Edit** then **Delete After Current Position** click **OK**.

▓ Use the **File - Save As** command to save the shortened file under a different name.

Copying one sound file into another

▓ To copy the whole sound file, use the command: **Edit - Copy** or Ctrl **C**.

▓ Open the destination file then go to the place where you want to insert the sound file.

▓ **Edit - Paste Insert** or Ctrl **V**

⇨ *To retrieve the sound file as it exists on the disk, use the **File - Revert** command, and click **Yes** to confirm.*

Recording your voice with a microphone

▓ Create a new file using **File - New**.

▓ Check that your microphone is switched on and properly connected to your PC, then press ⏺.

▓ Speak your text into the microphone then click ■.

▓ Save the file.

⇨ *You cannot record for more then 60 seconds.*

⇨ *If an audio CD is playing at the same time as your voice recording, the music will be recorded as background music to your words.*

Recording from an audio CD

▨ From the **Sound Recorder** application, create a new file.

▨ Start playing the audio CD with the **Windows Media Player** application.

▨ Make sure you can see both application windows then click the [●] button on the Sound Recorder to start recording.

The recording time allowed is limited to 60 seconds.

▨ If necessary, save the extract.

Mixing two sound files

You may, for example, wish to mix a CD and a recording of your voice.

▨ Activate one of the sound files (eg. the CD) and go to the point where you want to mix in the other.

▨ **Edit - Mix with File**

▨ Double-click the other sound file.

▨ Listen to the mixed file to check that you are satisfied with the result.

▨ If you need to, save the file under a new name.

⇨ *You can obtain a similar result simply by playing an audio CD while you are making a voice recording.*

⇨ *You can also copy into the clipboard the shorter of the files you are going to mix then use **Edit - Paste Mix** in the destination file.*

Increasing the recording time

You go beyond the usual 60 seconds of recording time.

▨ Once you have created a new file, make a white-noise recording: click the [●] button, and let the slider run through the allocated time, without recording anything.

▨ Next, copy this blank file using **Edit - Copy**.

▨ Create a new file.

▨ Click [●] and let the slider run to the end.

▨ Use the **Edit - Paste Insert** command to insert the first blank file from the clipboard.

You now have a recording that is double the usual maximum length.

▨ Click [◀◀] to record over the blank files, or you can even paste the file from the clipboard again.

⇨ *Be careful: if you paste several files together, the resulting document quickly becomes too large to manage.*

⇨ *The **Edit - Audio Properties** command allows you to set options for the various sound devices.*

3.6 Other applications

A-Using the Calculator

▧ To start the Calculator application, use **Start - Programs - Accessories - Calculator.**

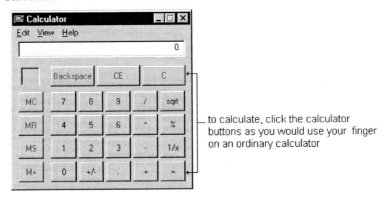

to calculate, click the calculator buttons as you would use your finger on an ordinary calculator

▧ To change the mode used, open the **View** menu then choose either **Scientific** or **Standard**.

⇨ *You can use the calculator from the keyboard, as each specific calculator button has a corresponding key or key combination.*

Calculating statistics

▧ With the calculator in scientific mode, click the **Sta** button.

The Statistics Box appears in the foreground.

▧ Drag the **Statistics Box** to move it, if necessary.

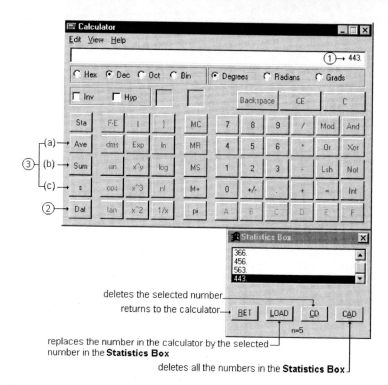

deletes the selected number

returns to the calculator

replaces the number in the calculator by the selected
number in the **Statistics Box**

deletes all the numbers in the **Statistics Box**

① Display the value in the calculator window.

② Enter the value in the **Statistics Box**.

③ After all the values are entered, click the calculator button that
performs the intended calculation:

(a)   to calculate an average.

(b)   to calculate a sum.

(c)   to calculate a standard deviation.

The result appears in the calculator window.

Activate the **Statistics Box** then click ☒ to close it.

B-Creating a document in several languages

*You can create a document using several different languages, by using
the keyboard language indicator at the end of the taskbar:*

keyboard language indicator

Configuring the keyboard language indicator

*If the keyboard language indicator does not appear on the taskbar or if it
does not contain the language you wish to use, you must change its
configuration.*

■ Go to the **Control Panel**, double-click the **Keyboard** icon and click the **Language** tab.

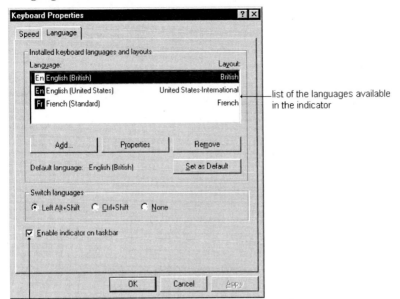

list of the languages available in the indicator

this option must be active for the indicator to appear on the taskbar

■ To add a language, click the **Add** button, choose the **Language** you wish to add from the list then click **OK**.

■ Click **OK** again to close the **Keyboard Properties** dialog box.

Composing a document

■ Go into the application in which you wish to compose your document (WordPad, Notepad, Microsoft Word, Microsoft Excel etc) and if necessary, create a new document or open an existing one to enter the required text.

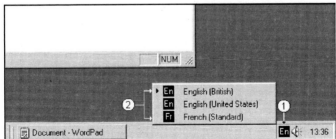

① Click the indicator to change language.

② Select the required language.

The regional settings for the chosen language instantly take effect. If for example you choose French, the keyboard layout changes from QWERTY to AZERTY.

Each time you wish to change language, click the keyboard language indicator and choose a different language.

C-Using the On-Screen Keyboard

This application displays a virtual keyboard on the screen so that users with limited mobility can enter data using an input device or joystick, rather than the keyboard.

Start - Programs - Accessories - Accessibility - On-Screen Keyboard

If you do not want to see the initial dialog box each time you start the On-Screen Keyboard, activate the **Do not show this message again** option then click **OK**.

If necessary, open the application in which you want to use the On-Screen Keyboard.

You can move the On-Screen Keyboard around by dragging its title bar. By default, the On-Screen Keyboard uses a "click to select" typing mode.

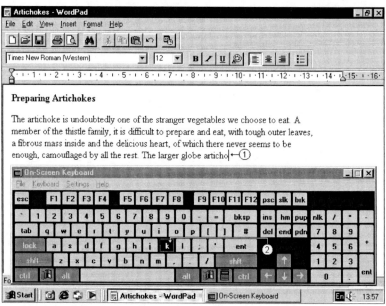

① Position the insertion point in the document.

② Click the required character to insert it into your document.

⇨ *When you point to a given character, it is highlighted.*

Modifying the layout of the On-Screen Keyboard

░ Open the **Keyboard** menu and choose from the following options:

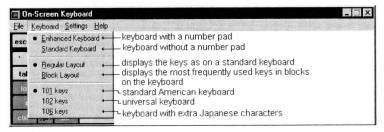

⇨ *The 102 keys and 106 keys options are not available in Block Layout.*

Changing the input mode

░ Open the **Settings** menu and choose **Typing Mode.**

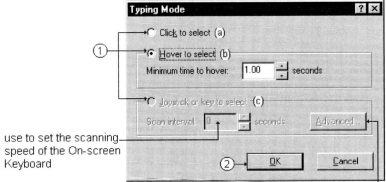

① Activate one of the following options:

(a)   activates the default **clicking mode.**

(b)   activates **hovering mode**: when the mouse pointer stays on a character for longer than the **Minimum time to hover**, the character is selected and inserted into the document.

(c)   activates **scanning mode**: each row of keys then each character on each row is scanned.

② Click to confirm the settings.

░ Click in the document at the place where you want to insert the next character and continue entering your text. If you are using scanning mode with a keyboard key, press that key to start the keyboard scan.

⇨ *To change the appearance of the keys of the On-Screen Keyboard, use Settings - Font and choose in which font you wish the keys to be displayed.*

⇨ *To hear a sound when you enter a character with the On-Screen Keyboard, activate the Use Click Sound option in the Settings menu.*

⇨ *To hide the On-Screen Keyboard when you toggle from one program to another, deactivate the Always On Top option in the Settings menu.*

D-Using the Magnifier

This application makes it easier for visually-impaired users to read information on the screen.

▦ **Start - Programs - Accessories - Accessibility - Magnifier**

A separate window appears at the top of the screen showing a close-up view of the part of the screen to which you are pointing.

▦ Define the Magnifier options:

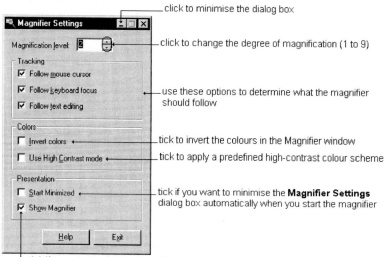

click to minimise the dialog box

click to change the degree of magnification (1 to 9)

use these options to determine what the magnifier should follow

tick to invert the colours in the Magnifier window

tick to apply a predefined high-contrast colour scheme

tick if you want to minimise the **Magnifier Settings** dialog box automatically when you start the magnifier

tick if you want to start the Magnifier and display the **Magnifier Settings** dialog box simultaneously

▦ To change the height of the magnification window, move the pointer onto its edge (the pointer takes the shape of a black double-headed arrow) and drag the edge of the window up or down.

▦ To change the location of the magnification window, place the pointer inside the window (the pointer takes the shape of a hand) and drag the window to the required place.

▦ To leave the Magnifier application, close the **Magnifier Settings** dialog box.

3.7 System tools

A-Defragmenting a drive

Defragmenting consists of grouping together the data on contiguous tracks on the disk so that data access is easier and faster.

▥ **Start - Programs - Accessories - System Tools - Disk Defragmenter** or, from the Explorer, right-click the disk drive, choose **Properties** then click the **Defragment Now** button on the **Tools** page.

*If you started the Disk Defragmenter with the **Programs - Accessories - System Tools** menu, a dialog box appears asking you to specify which drive should be defragmented.*

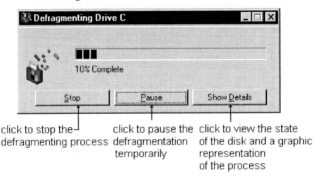

click to stop the   click to pause the click to view the state
defragmenting process defragmentation   of the disk and a graphic
                            temporarily   representation
                                                      of the process

APPLICATIONS

Defragmenting a hard drive can take more than an hour, depending on the state of the drive.
During defragmentation, you can still use your computer for other tasks, although it will work more slowly.

▥ At the end of the process, click **Yes** to start defragmenting another drive or click **No** to finish.

B-Creating a startup disk

You can use this disk to restart Windows should a problem occur.

▥ Go to the **Control Panel**.

▥ Double-click the **Add/Remove Programs** icon.

▥ Click the **Startup Disk** tab.

▥ Insert a blank formatted floppy disk into the drive then click the **Create Disk** button.

When the system files have been copied, Windows suggests you place a "Windows Millennium Edition Startup Disk" label on the floppy disk.

▥ Follow this advice then click **OK**.

C-Displaying the system information

The system information can supply useful information about the configuration of your computer.

▨ **Start - Programs - Accessories - System Tools - System Information**

The system information is divided into different categories called nodes and is organised in hierarchical form.

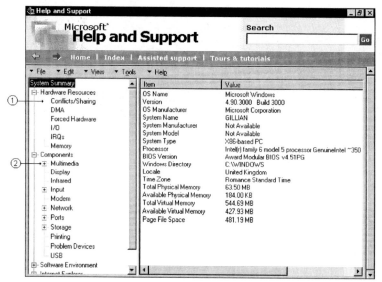

① Expand a branch by clicking the + sign in front of the node name.

② Click the node's name to view its contents in the right pane of the window.

*The **System Summary** node displays information pertaining to the computer and the version of the Windows Me operating system.*

*The **Hardware Resources** node shows settings specific to the hardware being used.*

*The **Components** node contains information about your configuration of Windows and can also indicate the status of any device drivers, network or multimedia applications.*

*The **Software Environment** node gives an overview of the software loaded in the computer.*

*The **Internet Explorer 5** node displays information concerning Internet Explorer 5.*

*The **Applications** node displays information specific to each application installed on your computer.*

Looking for system data

▓ **Edit - Find** or Ctrl **F**

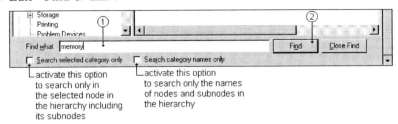

├── activate this option
│   to search only in
│   the selected node in
│   the hierarchy including
│   its subnodes

├── activate this option
│   to search only the names
│   of nodes and subnodes in
│   the hierarchy

① Enter the keyword(s) corresponding to the system information you are looking for.

② Click to start the search.

When Windows comes across the keyword, it stops and highlights the corresponding line.

▓ Continue searching with the **Find** button or click **Close Find** to interrupt the search.

Saving system information as a text file

It is possible to transfer the system information into a text editor, so as to send it to another person by email, for example.

▓ Select the category whose information you wish to save.

▓ **File - Export**

▓ Use the **Save in** box to specify where you wish to store the file.

▓ Enter a name for the text file in the **File name** box.

▓ Click the **Save** button.

Printing system information

▓ If required, select the node whose information you wish to print.

▓ **File - Print** or Ctrl **P**

▓ In the **Print range** frame, choose what you wish to print: the **All** option prints all the system information, the **Pages** option can be used to print a group of pages and the **Selection** option prints any selected node along with its subnodes. Click **OK** to print.

D-Cleaning up a disk

This tool detects and removes temporary files in order to free space on your hard disk (or on a floppy disk).

▓ **Start - Programs - Accessories - System Tools - Disk Cleanup**, or from the Windows Explorer, right-click the disk drive, choose **Properties** and the **General** tab and click **Disk Cleanup**.

▓ If you used the Start menu and not the Explorer, specify which drive you want to clean up: **A:** or **C:**.

The tool inspects the disk to look for the space to be cleaned up. A moment later, a dialog box appears, telling you how many bytes you can gain.

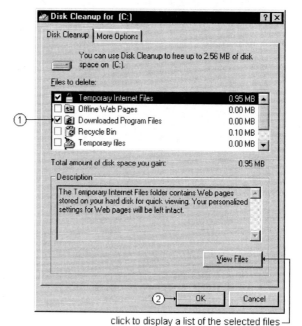

click to display a list of the selected files ⏌

① Select the type(s) of file you wish to erase by clicking the corresponding check box(es).
② Click to erase the selected files from the disk then confirm the file deletion.

E- Using the Character Map

This application provides a set of special and enhanced characters that you can insert in any Windows application. If the Character Map does not appear with the system tools, install the corresponding Windows component (cf. Installing/uninstalling Windows components).

▒ **Start - Programs - Accessories - System Tools - Character Map**

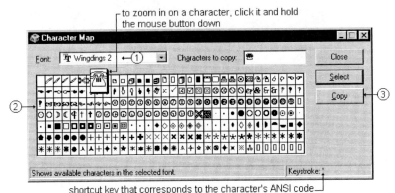

① Select the font containing the character you require.

② Double-click the character you want to insert (the character appears in the **Characters to copy** box).

③ Copy the contents of the **Characters to copy** box into the Windows clipboard.

▥ Go into the application then the document into which you wish to copy the character. Place the insertion point in the desired position.

▥ Click ▨ or use **Edit - Paste** to copy the contents of the clipboard into the active window.

⇨ *The inserted symbol is considered as a character: you can move it, delete it or change its size as with any other character.*

F-Using the task scheduler

Scheduled tasks allow you to programme the automatic execution of certain applications. The Scheduled Tasks utility opens at the same time as Windows and works in the background.

▥ **Start - Programs - Accessories - System Tools - Scheduled Tasks**

Creating a scheduled task

▥ From the **Scheduled Tasks** window, double-click the **Add Scheduled Task** icon.

The Scheduled Task Wizard opens and offers to help you.

▥ Click the **Next** button.

▥ Select the program you want Windows to run automatically then click **Next**.

APPLICATIONS

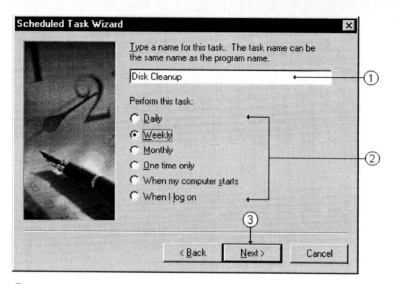

① If required, specify a name for this new task.

② Choose how often you want this task to be carried out.

③ Click to go to the next step.

▒ Depending on the option chosen in the previous step, give the day, time or frequency of execution if necessary then click **Next**.

▒ Click the **Finish** button.

The created task appears in the Scheduled Tasks window: the selected application will run automatically according to the settings you defined.

Modifying a scheduled task

▒ In the **Scheduled Tasks** window, click the task that you wish to modify.

▒ **File - Properties**

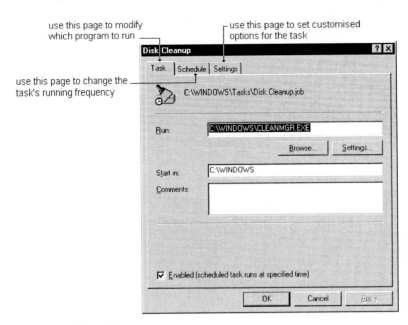

use this page to modify which program to run

use this page to set customised options for the task

use this page to change the task's running frequency

▓ Make the desired changes.

Deleting a scheduled task

▓ Open the **Scheduled Tasks** window and select the task you wish to delete.

▓ **File - Delete** or ⌧

▓ Confirm deleting the task.

⇨ *You can also right-click the task you wish to remove and choose the Delete option then confirm deleting the task.*

Deactivating the task scheduler

▓ Go into the **Scheduled Tasks** window.

▓ **Advanced - Stop Using Task Scheduler**

The defined tasks will no longer run and the Scheduled Tasks utility will not start at the same time as Windows.

⇨ *To deactivate the task scheduler temporarily, click the Pause Task Scheduler option in the Advanced menu. When you want to resume running all tasks, activate the Continue Task Scheduler option in the Advanced menu.*

⇨ *You must have administrator permissions to deactivate the task scheduler.*

4.1 Toolbars

A-Managing the taskbar

▒ Drag the taskbar to move it around the screen.

▒ To change its height (or width) point to the top edge (or the left edge) and drag.

▒ To determine how the taskbar appears on the screen, right-click a space on it and choose **Properties,** or activate the **Start - Settings - Taskbar and Start Menu** command and choose from the following options:

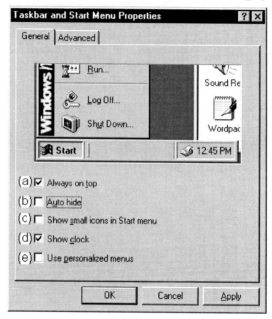

(a)   so that the bar stays on the screen even when the active application is displayed full screen.

(b)   minimises the taskbar to a line at the bottom of the screen. When you point to this line, the taskbar appears automatically and you can use it as usual.

(c)   reduces the size of the icons displayed in the **Start** menu.

(d)   displays the time in the status area on the taskbar. When you point to the clock, the control date appears in a ScreenTip.

(e)   activates the Personalized Menus function: applications that are used infrequently are hidden in the **Programs** menu.

B-Showing/hiding a toolbar

▓ Right-click an empty space on the taskbar.

▓ Activate the **Toolbars** option then one of the four toolbars offered: **Address, Links, Desktop** or **Quick Launch**.

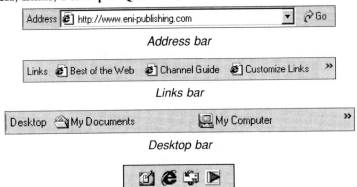

Address bar

Links bar

Desktop bar

Quick Launch bar

⇨ *By default, only the **Quick Launch** bar is shown.*

⇨ *When only part of a toolbar is shown, access the hidden icons by clicking the*  *button that appears on the right of the toolbar.*

C-Moving a toolbar/a tool within a bar

▓ To move a toolbar, point to the vertical line at the beginning of the toolbar you wish to move.

The mouse pointer becomes a black two-headed arrow.

▓ Drag it along the taskbar to the required place.

If you move a toolbar onto the desktop, it appears in its own separate window.

▓ To move a tool within a toolbar, click the tool you wish to move and without releasing the mouse, drag it left or right to the required position on the toolbar.

A thick black line indicates the tool's new position.

CONFIGURATION

D-Creating a toolbar

You can create two types of toolbar: one showing the contents of a folder, the other showing the contents of a Web site (in this case you should increase the height of the taskbar).

▨ Right-click an empty space on the taskbar.

▨ Activate **Toolbars** then the **New Toolbar** option.

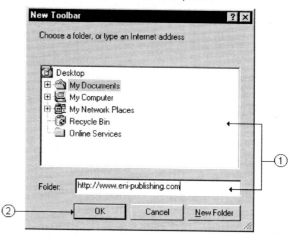

① Select a folder or enter an Internet address in the **Folder** text box.

② Confirm creating the toolbar.

⇨ *To hide (and at the same time delete) a created toolbar, deactivate the option corresponding to its name in the **Toolbars** shortcut menu.*

E-Creating a shortcut in a toolbar

*A shortcut represents an object such as a folder, an application or a file. It can be inserted as a tool button, especially the **Quick Launch** bar, so that you can access the file, folder or application quickly, directly from the toolbar.*

▨ Go into the **Explorer** window.

▨ Drag the icon from the folder, application or file directly onto the appropriate place on the desired toolbar (make sure the toolbar is visible first).

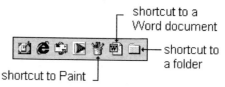

⇨ *To start the application symbolised by the shortcut or to open the represented folder or file, click the shortcut icon.*

4.2 The Start menu

A-Clearing the Documents menu

The Documents menu contains the names of the last fifteen files used.

▨ Right-click an empty space on the taskbar and choose **Properties**.

▨ On the **Advanced** page, click the **Clear** button then click **OK**.

B-Customising the Start menu

▨ Right-click an empty space on the taskbar and choose **Properties**.

▨ Click the **Advanced** tab.

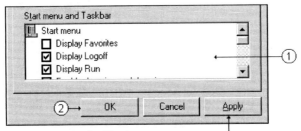

opens the **Start** menu so you can ⅃
check the effect produced

① Tick the options corresponding to what you wish to add to the **Start** menu.

② Click to confirm your changes.

C-Inserting an option into the Start menu

You can add options to the Start menu for easy access to your applications and the files you are working on.

First method

▨ Drag the file, application or folder icon onto the **Start** button on the taskbar: hold down the mouse and wait for the **Start** menu to open.
Drag the option into the required position in the menu. To add it to one of the submenus of the **Start** menu, drag it onto the option which opens the submenu and then into postition.

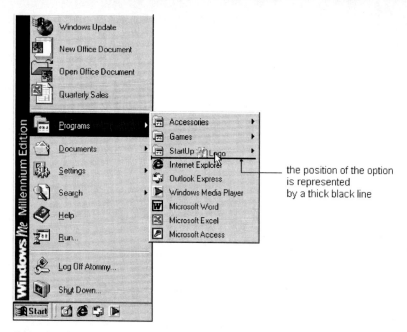

the position of the option
is represented
by a thick black line

▓ Once the option is in a suitable position, release the mouse button.

⇨ *You can simply, drag the icon representing the file, application or folder onto the **Start** button. In this case the new option will appear in the top section of the **Start** menu (like the Quarterly Sales spreadsheet in the illustration).*

Second method

▓ Right-click an empty space on the taskbar and choose **Properties**.

▓ Click the **Advanced** tab then the **Add** button.

▓ Give the full name of the object you want to insert in the **Start** menu: if it is a file, give its name; if it is an application, give the name of the corresponding program file. Use the **Browse** button to check in the hierarchy.

A program file is an executable file; double-clicking this type of file opens the corresponding application. This type of file has an EXE, COM or BAT extension.

▓ Click **Next**.

▓ Click the **Start Menu** icon to tell Windows that the option corresponding to the program or the file should be inserted in the **Start** menu.

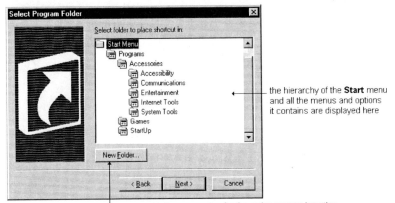

the hierarchy of the **Start** menu and all the menus and options it contains are displayed here

you can create a new menu for the option you are inserting

- Click **Next** and give the option name you want to see in the **Start** menu.
- Click **Finish** then **OK**.

Third method

- In the **Explorer**, open the **C:\WINDOWS** folder then open the **Start Menu** folder.

- To create a new option in the **Start** menu, copy the document, program file or shortcut concerned into the **Start Menu** folder. To create a new option in the **Programs** submenu or a lower-level submenu, start by opening the **Programs** folder.

the submenus and options in the Programs menu appear here

*This folder corresponds to the **Programs** menu in the **Start** menu. It contains any shortcuts you may have inserted (you will notice that shortcuts are associated with this icon:* ▨).

▨ Copy the appropriate file into the **Programs** folder or into one of the submenu folders (**Accessories, Games, StartUp**...).

⇨ *With the **Programs** menu open, you can drag its options to new positions in the menu or into the submenus. This also works for the options in the submenus.*

D-Inserting a submenu into the Start menu

▨ Right-click an empty space on the taskbar and choose **Properties**.

▨ Click the **Advanced** tab then the **Add** button.

▨ Select the program file, or document that corresponds to it in the first option of the submenu then click **Next**.

▨ Click the menu folder into which you are going to insert the new menu then click **New Folder**.

*A folder called **Program Group (1)** is created.*

▨ Enter the name of the menu.

▨ If necessary, give the name of the first option in the submenu.

▨ Click **Finish** then **OK**.

▨ Click the **Start** button then open the **Programs** menu to check that the submenu has been created.

⇨ *Of course, another way to insert a submenu is to create its folder in the Explorer and insert the shortcuts corresponding to the options you want to see in the menu.*

⇨ *To open a file, folder or application automatically when Windows starts, copy the item into the StartUp menu in Start - Programs.*

E-Removing options from the Start menu

First method

▨ Right-click an empty space on the taskbar and choose **Properties**.

▨ Click the **Advanced** tab then the **Remove** button.

▨ Select the item you intend to remove then click the **Remove** button.

▨ Repeat this procedure for each item you wish to remove.

▨ Click **Close** then **OK**.

Second method

▨ Go into the Explorer and open the **Start Menu** folder located inside the **C:\WINDOWS** folder.

▨ Delete the folders and files corresponding to the menus or options you wish to remove. Confirm the removal with **OK**.

4.3 The interface

A-Displaying the desktop as a Web page

You can activate Windows' Active Desktop function, which allows you to customise your desktop with an active element, namely an automatically refreshed Web page.

▦ To activate the Active Desktop feature, go into the **Control Panel** and double-click the **Display** icon.

▦ Click the **Web** tab then activate the **Show Web content on my Active Desktop** option.

▦ Click the **New** button.

▦ In the **Location** box, enter the URL address of the Web page you wish to use or click the **Browse** button to look for it.

the chosen Web page appears on the desktop ⌐

⇨ *You can also add Web content to the desktop by right-clicking any empty space on the desktop and choosing **Active Desktop** then **New Desktop Item**. Enter the URL address of the Web page you wish to display or use the **Browse** button to look for it.*

⇨ *If you no longer wish to display a Web page on the desktop, right-click an empty space on the desktop, go to the Active Desktop option and deactivate the Show Web Content option.*

B-Activating Single-click/Double-click mode

You may remember that the file selection techniques used in the Windows Explorer differ depending on the active working mode, which by default is Double-click mode.

▓ Go into the **Control Panel** and double-click the **Folder Options** then click the **General** tab, if necessary.

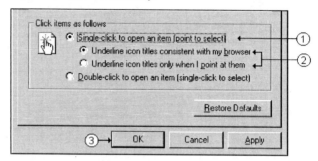

① Activate this option to activate Single-click mode.

② Select how you wish to underline icon titles.

③ Click to confirm.

⇨ *To return to Double-click mode, activate the Double-click to open an item option in the Folder Options dialog box (General tab).*

C-Activating the Personalized Menus feature

This Windows Me feature hides infrequently used items in the Programs menu.

▓ **Start - Settings - Taskbar and Start Menu**

▓ Activate the **Use Personalized Menus** option on the **General** page then click **OK**.

⇨ *When this feature is active, you can still access the hidden applications by clicking the arrow at the bottom of the Programs menu.*

D-Creating a shortcut on the desktop

A shortcut represents an object such as a document, a program or a drive. It can be inserted on the desktop so that the document, application or drive is accessible as soon as you go into Windows.

▨ Start the Explorer, but do not display the window full screen: part of the desktop should be visible in the background.

▨ Drag the icon of the document, the program or the folder onto the desktop.

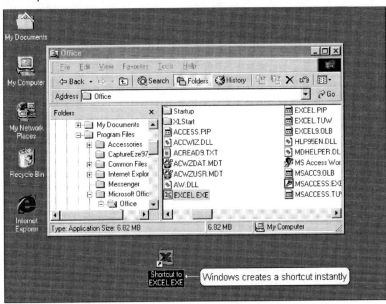

▨ A double-click on the shortcut icon runs the application, or opens the folder or document.

⇨ *To delete a shortcut, right-click it and choose the **Delete** option. Confirm the deletion.*

E-Managing icons on the desktop

▨ To move icons, drag them across the desktop.

▨ To line them up on the same axis, right-click an empty space close to the axis you have in mind, and take the **Line Up Icons** option.

▨ To arrange the icons in order, right-click a space on the desktop, open the **Arrange Icons** menu and indicate in what order they should appear.

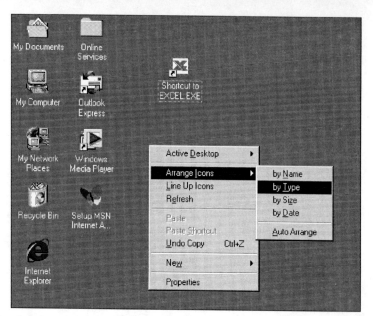

To change an icon's name, click the name twice, modify it then press `Enter`.

To change the look of the icons, right-click an empty space on the desktop, click the **Properties** option then the **Effects** tab. Select the item whose icon you wish to change then click the **Change Icon** button. Click **OK**.

⇨ *You can also use the **Default Icon** button (in the **Display Properties** dialog box, **Effects** tab) to return to using the default icon for the selected item.*

F-Changing the desktop's background

Right-click an empty space on the desktop and click the **Properties** option.

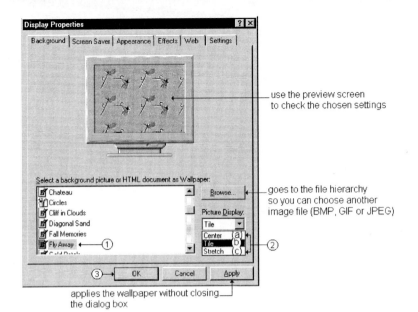

use the preview screen
to check the chosen settings

goes to the file hierarchy
so you can choose another
image file (BMP, GIF or JPEG)

applies the wallpaper without closing
the dialog box

① Select the image you wish to display over the desktop.

② Choose how to arrange the image on the background:

(a)   The single image appears at the centre of the screen.

(b)   The image is duplicated until it fills the whole screen.

(c)   The single image is blown up to fill the whole screen.

③ Enter.

⇨ *You can also select wallpaper from Paint or from a Web page if you are connected to the Internet.*

G-Choosing a screen saver

A screen saver feature displays a picture (often an animated image) on the screen when your computer lies idle for a given time. This ensures a longer life for the lights in your monitor.

▓ Right-click an empty space on the desktop then click the **Properties** option.

▓ Click the **Screen Saver** tab.

contains options for icon management

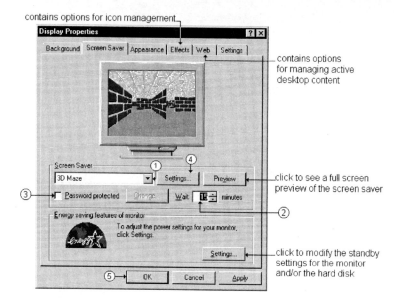

contains options
for managing active
desktop content

click to see a full screen
preview of the screen saver

click to modify the standby
settings for the monitor
and/or the hard disk

① Select a screen saver.

② Specify, in minutes, how long the computer should be inactive before the screen saver starts.

③ Activate this option to associate your log on password with the screen saver (this password will be requested before the Windows screen reappears).

④ Click this button to set parameters for the chosen screen saver (if you have chosen **3D Text** for example, you can enter the text you want the screen saver to display).

⑤ Click to confirm.

⇨ *Do not confuse the screen saver with the screen standby feature, whose main goal is to save energy.*

H-Defining the appearance of windows and dialog boxes

▓ Right-click an empty space on the desktop and click the **Properties** option.

▓ Click the **Appearance** tab.

▓ Select one of the default **Schemes** proposed.

▓ To change the colour of one of the desktop features, select an **Item** from the list and choose new colours in the appropriate drop-down lists.

▓ To change the size of one of the desktop items, select the **Item** in the list and use the **Size** list box to choose a new size.

▓ If the selected item contains text, you can change the **Font**, the font **Size** and its **Color** or even show it in bold and/or italic type.

If you wish to save these parameters as a new scheme, click the **Save As** button and give a name to your new scheme.

Click **OK**.

I- Setting screen display parameters

Click the **Settings** tab.

Select the number of **Colors** used on the screen.

The options in the Colors list are directly linked to the characteristics of your graphics card.

If required, you can change the screen resolution by dragging the **Screen area** slider.

The screen resolution determines the number of pixels displayed over the width and height of the screen. A large number of pixels means that the elements on the screen are smaller so you can display more elements at any given time.

Click **OK**.

J- Associating sounds with events

Open the **Control Panel** folder and start the application called **Sounds and Multimedia**.

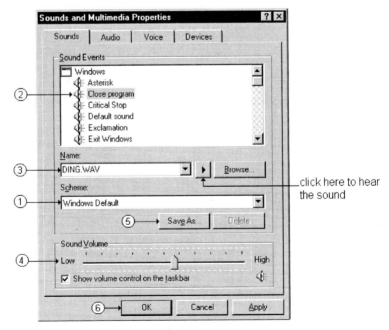

click here to hear the sound

① If you want to, choose a sound scheme.

② Select the event to which you are associating the sound.

③ Choose the sound document to run when the event occurs.

④ If you wish, adjust the volume by dragging the slider.

⑤ If you do not wish to modify the active scheme, click this button to save the scheme under another name.

⑥ Click to confirm.

K-Changing the control date

▓ To set the date and time, double-click the time displayed on the taskbar, or run the **Date/Time** application from the **Control Panel**.

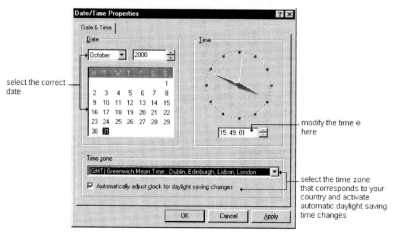

select the correct date

modify the time e here

select the time zone that corresponds to your country and activate automatic daylight saving time changes

L-Defining regional settings for dates and numbers

▓ From the **Control Panel**, run the **Regional Settings** application.

▓ Under the **Regional Settings** tab, click the region whose settings you require.

▓ Use the **Numbers** page to define the format of numerical values in Windows applications.

use this page to manage currency formats

use these pages to control time and date formats

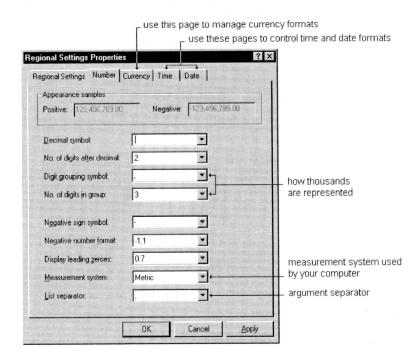

how thousands are represented

measurement system used by your computer

argument separator

M-Defining how the mouse is used

In the **Control Panel** window, double-click the **Mouse** icon.

options for pointer presentation

options concerning pointer movement

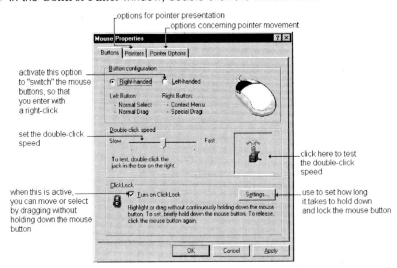

activate this option to "switch" the mouse buttons, so that you enter with a right-click

set the double-click speed

when this is active, you can move or select by dragging without holding down the mouse button

click here to test the double-click speed

use to set how long it takes to hold down and lock the mouse button

CONFIGURATION

N-Managing fonts

▓ Open the **Fonts** folder in the **Control Panel**.

▓ Define the presentation of this window in the **View** menu; the **List Fonts by Similarity** option compares all the fonts to a reference font, which you select, and lists them in order of their similarity to it.

▓ A double-click on a font icon opens a window, where you can see examples of characters in this font at different sizes (the **Print** button prints the contents of this window).

▓ To delete a font, delete the corresponding item.

▓ To install a font, use the **File - Install New Font** command then select the drive and the folder where the font files are stored. Select the fonts you wish to install, holding down the ⬆ Shift and Ctrl keys as necessary, then click **OK**.

▓ 4.4 Installation

A-Configuring/installing hardware

▓ Double-click the **Add New Hardware** icon in the **Control Panel** then click **Next** twice.

▓ If the hardware is physically installed on your computer, leave the **Yes (Recommended)** option active then click **Next** twice.

▓ When the search for new devices is complete, click **Next**.

▓ If the hardware has not yet been installed, select the type of device you are installing and click **Next**.

Depending on what you are installing, an extra dialog box may appear.

▓ Set the options as required then click **Next**.

▓ Choose the manufacturer then the required model.

▓ Click **Have Disk** so Windows can copy the device driver from the floppy disk or CD-ROM supplied with the device.

▓ Follow the instructions until the installation is complete.

B-Installing a printer

Installing a local printer

▓ Open the **Printers** folder with the **Start - Settings - Printers** command or via the **Control Panel**.

▓ Double-click the **Add Printer** icon then click the **Next** button.

▓ Activate the **Local printer** option then click **Next**.

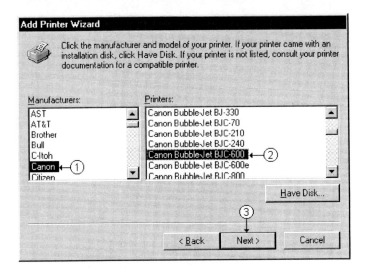

① Choose the name of the printer's manufacturer.

② Select the model you are using.

③ Click to continue the process.

▓ Select the port where the printer is connected then click **Next**.

▓ If you wish, change the **Printer name** and specify whether this should be the default printer used in your applications then click **Next**.

▓ Indicate whether or not you wish to print a test page (this is generally a good idea) and click **Finish**.

Installing a network printer

▓ Open the **Printers** folder with the **Start - Settings - Printers** command or via the **Control Panel**.

▓ Double-click the **Add Printer** icon then click the **Next** button.

▓ Activate the **Network printer** option then click **Next**.

▓ Enter the printer name or click **Browse** to look for the printer if you do not know its name.

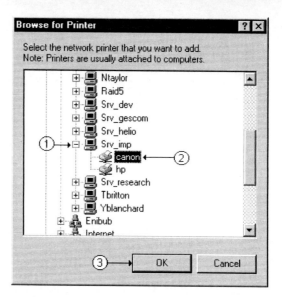

① Double-click the name of the server or workstation containing the printer you wish to install.

② Click the name of the printer to be installed.

③ Click to continue.

▨ Specify whether or not applications should use this as the default printer then click **Next** and finally click **Finish**.

C-Installing/uninstalling an application

Installing an application

▨ Go to the **Control Panel** and double-click the **Add/Remove Programs** icon.

▨ On the **Install/Uninstall** page, click the **Install** button.

▨ As prompted by Windows, insert the first installation floppy disk or first CD-ROM in the drive and click **Next**.

*Windows searches the floppy disk and CD-ROM drives for the installation program then displays the program's name in the **Command line for installation program** box. The **Browse** button can be used to make a manual search for the installation program.*

▨ Click the **Finish** button to start the installation. Follow the various steps of the program installation through to the end.

⇨ *When the program is installed, its name appears in the **Programs** menu, from where it can be run.*

⇨ *You can also use the **Run** option in the **Start** menu to install a program from a floppy disk or CD-ROM.*

Modifying/removing an application

▓ Go to the **Control Panel** and double-click the **Add/Remove Programs** icon.

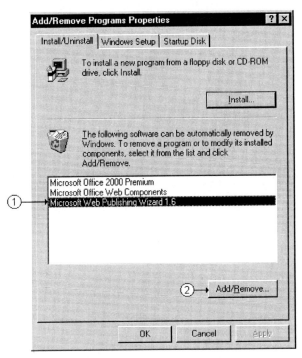

① Click the line that corresponds to the application you want to change or remove.

② Click this button. Be careful: this button sometimes deletes an application without leaving you the option of simply modifying it.

▓ Follow the instructions given to change or uninstall the program in question.

D-Installing/uninstalling Microsoft Office 2000 applications

Installing one or more Microsoft Office 2000 applications

▓ Place the first Microsoft Office 2000 CD-ROM in the drive and wait for the installation process to start.

You can also start the installation from the Control Panel, using the Add/Remove Programs option or with the Start - Run command.

▓ Enter your **Customer Information** and click **Next**.

▓ Activate the **I accept the terms in the License Agreement** option and click **Next**.

- To make a default installation, click the **Install Now** button.

Windows asks you to wait and displays the Installing Microsoft Office 2000 dialog box. You will have to restart your computer so Windows can complete the Microsoft Office 2000 setup.

- To make a different installation from the one proposed by default, click the **Customize** button.
- If necessary, use the **Browse** button to change the folder where the Office programs will be installed then click **Next**.

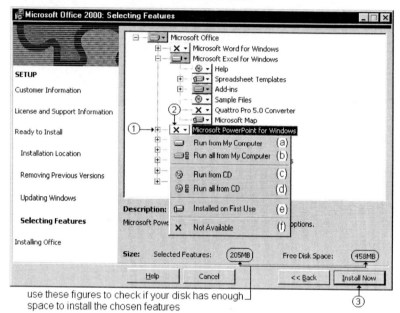

use these figures to check if your disk has enough space to install the chosen features

① Select which features you want to install. Click the + (plus) sign to expand a feature (if you do not want to install everything).

② To change the way a feature is installed, click its icon then choose another option:

(a)   to install and store the feature on your hard disk.

(b)   to install and store the feature and all its subfeatures on your hard disk.

(c)   to install the feature from the CD-ROM: the application is not copied onto your hard disk and all the files required to use the application stay on the CD-ROM. You will always need the Microsoft Office 2000 CD-ROM to use this application.

(d)   to install the feature and all its subfeatures from the CD-ROM: the application is not copied onto your hard disk and all the files required to use the application stay on the CD-ROM. You will always need to Microsoft Office 2000 CD-ROM to use this application.

(e)   to install the feature on your hard disk when you use it for the first time. When that occurs, you will need to go to the Microsoft Office 2000 CD-ROM to install the feature.

(f)   not to install the feature.

③ When you have made all your choices for the installation, click to start the installation process.

Adding/removing Microsoft Office 2000 components

▒ Go to the **Control Panel** and double-click the **Add/Remove Programs** icon.

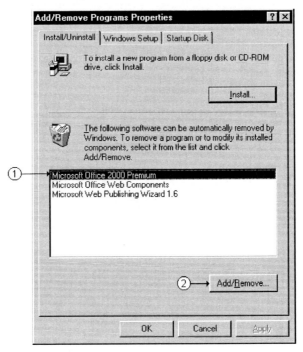

① Click this line.

② Click to modify the installation.

▒ Place the Microsoft Office 2000 CD-ROM in the drive and wait for the installation to start.

▒ In the **Microsoft Office 2000 Maintenance Mode** dialog box, click the **Add or Remove Features** button.

▒ Select the features you want to install or delete, as for the first installation. Be careful: if you untick any check box, that feature is automatically uninstalled!

▒ When your choice is complete, click the **Update Now** button to start the installation.

E- Installing/uninstalling Windows components

You can remove some components or add others that were not included when you first installed Windows Me.

▒ Go to the **Control Panel** then double-click the **Add/Remove Programs** icon.

▒ In the dialog box that appears, click the **Windows Setup** tab (if necessary).

After a brief wait, Windows displays a list of its components. Those whose check box is ticked are already installed on your computer.

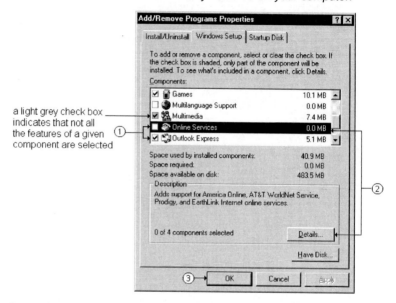

a light grey check box indicates that not all the features of a given component are selected ①

① To install a component in its entirety, tick its check box. To remove a component, click to remove the tick from its check box.

② To select certain parts of components that you wish to install or remove, click the component's name then the **Details** button. Activate or deactivate the component parts that you want to install or remove then click **OK**.

③ Click to continue the installation.

F- Installing a system language

▓ Go to the **Control Panel** and double-click the **Add/Remove Programs** icon.

▓ Go to the **Windows Setup** page.

▓ Tick the **Multilanguage Support** check box.

▓ If required, click the **Details** button if you wish to deactivate some language options and click **OK**.

▓ Insert the Windows Me CD-ROM and click **OK**.

General shortcut keys

F1	Display the **Help** window.
Alt F4	Leave an application.
⇧ Shift F10	Display a selection shortcut menu.
Ctrl Esc	Open the **Start** menu.
Alt ⇄	Activate an application that is already open.
Prt Sc	Copy the current screen image into the clipboard.
Alt Prt Sc	Copy the active window image into the clipboard.
Ctrl X	Cut the selection.
Ctrl C	Copy the selection.
Ctrl V	Paste the selection.
Ctrl Z	Undo the last action.
Ctrl A	Select all.

Windows Explorer

F2	Rename a folder or document.
F3	Display the **Search** explorer bar.
Del	Delete a folder or document.
⇧ Shift Del	Delete a file without sending it to the Recycle Bin.
Alt Enter	Display the selected object's properties.
F5	Refresh the window.
Alt ←	Display the previous page.
Alt →	Display the next page.
F6	Go from one pane to another.

Folders Explorer Bar open in the Explorer

*	Expand branch completely (folders and subfolders).
+	Expand a branch.
-	Collapse a branch.
→	Expand branch or, it is already expanded, select the first subfolder.
←	Collapse branch or, it is already collapsed, select the folder above.

Properties dialog box

Ctrl ⇄	Activate the next page.
Ctrl ⇧ Shift ⇄	Activate the previous page.

Open and Save As dialog boxes

F4	Open the **Look in** list.
F5	Refresh the dialog box contents.
←	If you have selected a folder, open the folder above.

A

ACCESSIBILITY

ACCESSING

ACCESSORIES

ACTION

APPLICATION

C

CALCULATOR

CAPTURE

CD

CHARACTER MAP

CLIP

CLIPBOARD

See also COPYING, MOVING

CLOSING

COLLECTION

COLOUR

COMPRESSED FOLDER

COMPUTER

CONFIGURATION

P

PAINT

See also COLOUR, DRAWING

PASSWORD

PREVIEW

PRINTER

PRINTING

PROGRAM

See APPLICATION

PROJECT

PROPERTIES

PROTECTION

R

RECORDING

RECYCLE BIN

REGIONAL SETTINGS

RENAMING

RETRIEVING

S

SAVING

SCHEDULED TASKS

INDEX

INDEX

publishing

VISIT OUR WEB SITE

www.eni-publishing.com

▲ **Quick Reference Guide**
▲ **User Manual**
▲ **Practical Guide**
▲ **Training CD-ROM**
▲ **Microsoft®**
   Approved Publication

Ask for our free brochure

For more information on our new titles please complete this card and return

Name: ....

....

Company: ....

Address: ....

....

Postcode: ....

Town: ....

Phone: ....

E-mail: ....

Please affix stamp here

ENI Publishing LTD

500 Chiswick High Road

London W4 5RG